COUNTRY CHRONICLE

By Gladys Taber

COUNTRY CHRONICLE

by Gladys Taber

Illustrations by PAMELA JOHNSON

J. B. LIPPINCOTT COMPANY
Philadelphia & New York

U.S. Library of Congress Cataloging in Publication Data

Taber, Gladys (Bagg), birth date
    Country chronicle.

    1.   Country life—Connecticut. 2.   Cookery.
I.   Title.
S521.5.C8T3   917.46   73-19684
ISBN-0-397-01023-0

For HUGH JOHNSON
Whose warm friendship and encouragement
have kept the lamp lighted over my desk
for more nights than I can remember

CONTENTS

ONCE UPON A TIME...

is the way most legends begin, and the phrase usually
ushers in the world of magic. Mine also begins once
upon a time on a day when the god of winter turned
all his battalions on a quiet valley in New England. The
wind blew, piling up knee-deep drifts, and the snow fell
in that curious swirling motion of a great blizzard. The
cold sliced the air like a carving knife.

The only sign of life was two figures, bent like
buttonhooks and struggling across what turned out in
due time to be a cornfield. Anyone feeling these two
were quite mad would have had no argument. The
realtor was a quarter of a mile back, on what was theoretically a road, trying to shovel his car out, and nobody
ever heard what he said.

But Jill and I had come out from the big city to
look at a house in the country, and we did not believe in
letting nature take its course if it interfered with ours.
It was too bad we had no boots, Jill observed. She was
wearing new black suede shoes, then the height of style,
and her passage was marked with great inky blobs as the
shoes gave in. (The dye was not permanent.)

The house we had come to see was a farmhouse

built around 1690, with twenty-eight acres more or less
as the deed went. It was off Jeremy Swamp Road and
the old Kettletown road, which went nowhere but had
once led to an early settlement called Kettletown, because the thrifty settlers bought it from the Indians for
a kettle.

After half an hour we could see the house dimly
through the snow, not a true salt-box but slant-roofed
and looking like a one-story building. It turned out to
have two stories, but Yankee thrift had made it look
like one, since in those days taxes were measured by
stories.

The realtor's last words to us as we left him were
"Sorry I don't have a key. Have to go in by the cellar
door."

Before dark we reached the house and found the
cellar door, which was *not* four feet deep in snow because the ell of the house had protected it. It was a big
slanting door and it was frozen shut, but Jill managed
to grab and heave one side while I stood on the other.
The stair well to the cellar was walled with great hand-
hewn granite blocks, and from the cellar to upstairs the
flight of steps looked like a misplaced ladder.

Of course we had no light, but we did have some
matches. We felt our way up the inside stairway through
cobwebs and came out in the keeping room, directly in
front of the great fireplace. A pale glimmer of daylight
came through the twelve-by-eight-inch paned windows.
The fireplace walls were also of hand-hewn stone, and
the great hearth was of flat blocks. The wrought-iron
crane was orange with rust, the Dutch-oven door
charred. But there it was!

The fireplace took up one whole wall of the long, narrow room. And there were five doors in the room, leaving little space for furniture. In the early days houses were built around a central chimney, and ours was fourteen feet square. One door led down the ladder-steep stairs to the cellar, one to the front parlor, one to a second parlor (which became my bedroom), one to the old milk room (which was to become the kitchen), and one to the upstairs. There were windows on two sides overlooking an old apple orchard and the ancient well house. I have often been asked to draw a map of the house but have never managed to make it plausible.

As we stood shivering, I looked at the floor. It was of hand-cut black oak with square hand-cut nails, but there were some holes here and there, which some former dweller had covered with flattened tin cigarette cases. Jill was admiring the great beamed ceiling and the walls, which were plastered with ancient plaster, rough and bumpy. The old plaster mix was held together by horsehairs and, so far as I know, cannot be imitated by today's plasterers.

One bubbly old pane of glass had a piece of plaster-board nailed over the cracks.

"This is it," I said as the last match went out.

So we signed the papers and bought it.

The next weekend was a kind of false spring, and we came out to look at the upstairs. Also came a man who had planned to buy the house but had stayed home when the weather was so bad. He offered to take it over for a great deal more than we had paid and seemed not to believe he could not have it.

"Good thing we came out in the blizzard," remarked Jill. "Good thing, too, we didn't know all the plumbing was cracked, and the pipes frozen solid."

And when we went to the village for some of those hot dogs Ralph Nader deplores, the lunch-counter man said, "Well, so you're the ladies who bought the old house on Jeremy Swamp Road. It's been empty a long time because of the murder and suicide. Supposed to be haunted. Want mustard or catsup?"

So along with the shabby, leaking, ancient house, we had acquired a murder and a suicide!

"If we have ghosts, I know they will be nice people," I said.

Why did we do it? Probably because we had dreamed of a house in the country for weekends, restful, sunny, carefree, a kind of Camelot. Or a permanent picnic among woods, wild flowers, singing birds, fresh country eggs, and creamy milk from a nearby farm. A haven for the children, three cocker spaniels, and one Siamese cat.

We grew up in small, quiet Midwestern towns, were college roommates at one of the Eastern colleges in a setting so lovely it seemed fictional. Jill went on to study in Vienna and married her doctor husband, who was coming home to New York City to practice. I went back to Wisconsin and married a young faculty member at what was then Lawrence College.

Eventually both families came to the city and faced the smog and noise and confusion and the problems of raising three small children in gloomy apartments. Jill's son, David, was four, her daughter, Barbara, six, and my daughter, Connie, eight. And one day as we walked the children along Central Park West, I looked up at the hazy sky and said, "If only we could get to the country for a weekend, the real country!"

"Even a small piece of land we could put tents on," said Jill.

Our husbands were dubious about the practicability but felt if we did work it out ourselves on our own, they might enjoy an occasional brook trout grilled over charcoal.

This is probably the end of the legend, for grim reality faced us as soon as we inspected the house with some care. There were an old coal-burning furnace and a rusty cast-iron range with a reservoir at one side filled with brownish water. All the plumbing fixtures were cracked, because nobody had ever bothered to drain the pipes in winter. There were a few pieces of antique pine and maple furniture, but most of the rooms were filled with piles of old rags and dead mice.

We simply did not have enough money to buy our dream house and hire a competent contractor to repair it.

"We'll just camp out," said Jill, "but a plumber will have to fix the bathroom and we must have a refrigerator."

"The children can help," I said.

It turned out the children did not like to mow lawns but were good at doing dishes and picking wild blackberries for supper. We also learned that David was allergic to any kind of pollen, and the girls were dearly loved by mosquitoes, bees, and wasps. All three suffered acutely from poison ivy the first summer. However, as soon as they stopped peeling from sunburn, they began to look brown and healthy and ate like the traditional farmhands. It was a great relief not to prepare separate menus for each one but to dish up a community meal.

The cockers, of course, tried to catch skunks, and Esmé, my Siamese, insisted on bringing in dead mice to lay on my bed.

As for us, no peasant in the Middle Ages in Europe ever worked harder. There were the times when we discovered we had put on a whole length of wallpaper upside down in David's room and when Jill painted herself into a corner of the front parlor, and I lighted a beautiful fire in the great fireplace but left the damper closed, which resulted in enough smoke pouring into the room to make it a disaster area.

We found that a very old house in the country does not encourage sitting under blossoming apple trees and sipping tall, cool drinks or strolling among the wild flowers in the upper woods. When we were in the yard, we were mowing or planting roses by the picket fence or trimming the lilacs. Also, a good many snakes had taken over when the house was uninhabited and had a habit of coming out of the swamp just as Jill was digging up the bed for the asparagus. Snakes were the one product of nature she was afraid of, so I was delegated to kill them. Since I am one who always walks around an ant to avoid killing and tries to scoop wasps up in pieces of Kleenex when they come into the house, I did not enjoy my job.

We kept a strong iron rake by the back door, which I grabbed when I heard Jill scream. The trick was to bring the back of the rake down on the snake just back of the head with a smashing blow—and spend the next few hours wondering why anyone should ever kill anything that was alive and minding his or her own business.

I was reminded of those days last winter when the plumber crawled in around the cellar pipes to fix a leak and reported gleefully that he found the skin of a five-foot black snake under the crawl space. It was not the kind of relic I wished to preserve.

Eventually the snakes that were still around moved back to the swamp. There are still a few friendly green snakes that like to hang around the old well house, but the big ones are gone. Our wildlife consists of skunks, raccoons, squirrels, and chipmunks, all of whom we feed patiently, along with the many birds. Occasionally there are a few ruffed grouse, but they are shy and stay at the extreme edge of the meadow.

As I look back at the early days at the farm, I sometimes wonder why we never were discouraged; addicts of country living can easily understand. Once you put down roots in your own place, you have a special awareness of how blessed you are. The feeling is compounded of many things, such as walking on dewy grass instead of pavements and watching a harvest moon rise over your very own swamp and bringing in your own fresh asparagus from the bed down by the pond. And hearing the stillness of an early morning. And breathing snow-pure air on a January day. And putting a log of wood from the fallen apple tree in the old orchard on the open fire.

But most special of all, perhaps, is the quality of light. The world is brighter away from the city. The sky is an immense arc of light, and even the darkness of great storms seems strangely luminous.

Measuring time, as I have said before, is an impossibility for me. Some days are years and some only a breath. But in the end, we did have Stillmeadow repaired and furnished with books and old pine and maple furniture—not to mention a garden full of vegetables. And later, at the time we lost our husbands, the city apartments were turned over to new tenants. Stillmeadow was our refuge as we adjusted to our personal losses, and it was amazing how well the old farmhouse accepted bits and pieces from the two city apartments without seeming overcrowded.

We settled in with a bevy of cockers, two Irish setters, a Siamese, and a Manx cat. We bought a hotel-sized freezer to help with the vegetables from Jill's garden, which grew bigger by the year. Jill's idea of happiness was five more rows of potatoes and a sweet-corn field bigger than any other in the neighborhood. Aside from freezing the surplus, we canned everything including squash, which at that time *Farm Journal* did not advise. We made applesauce, apple jelly, grape jelly from wild grapes, elderberry jelly, relishes, chutney, sauces.

The beans were almost our undoing. Any gardener will instantly understand this. Jill would come in, shedding garden loam at every step, and drop a basketful of beautiful tender green beans on the counter. "The blankety-blank beans are at it again!" she'd say.

Barbara fortunately came to the rescue, put down her book, and said, "I'll help with those beans."

While I snipped beans and more beans, I could see Jill's tall figure and Barbara's small, slim one bending over the bean rows, picking and picking and picking. We all liked beans within reason, but twice a day was too much. And when the corn was ripe, we had corn on the cob, roast corn, corn pudding, corn soufflé, corn chowder, and corn in mixed-vegetable salad.

But once a true gardener begins to *grow crops,* there is no stopping him or her. Our farm neighbors were generous, too, and often turned up with baskets of fat, rosy beets, pink-skinned onions, chard, and juicy tomatoes just as we were filling baskets with Jill's Mexican corn (streaked with blue) and crisp lettuce and cucumbers. Our favorite farm neighbor, Willie, brought sacks of potatoes from up the hill.

I cooked. Sometimes I felt the kitchen was the only room in the house, and I was always in it. (There was a side effect of this, for I began to collect recipes and write cookbooks.) And I learned that in the country you never know how many will drop in and stay for supper. It may be five; it may be ten.

When I did get out of the kitchen, I retired to the haymow in the barn to work at my trade of writing. With the sweet smell of long-ago hay and a view of meadows and hills through the great open doors through which loads of hay once came, I was happy.

Out of garden season, Jill refinished old pieces of furniture or built what we needed, such as a trestle table for the keeping room or a pine flat-topped desk for me or garden benches. The trestle table was her masterpiece, for it has a single solid piece of pine for the top and at a pinch will seat eight.

All the children helped with the cocker puppies we raised and, when we got the hens, carried in the warm fresh-laid eggs in time for breakfast every morning.

We were fortunate in having the Phillips farm

across the road (originally Philliponi from Lithuania).
The five children, especially the three boys, became
part of our lives. The oldest son, Frank, helped us first,
and my favorite memory of him is the day my Siamese,
Esmé, got to the top of one of the giant sugar maples
and froze there. Frank was unloading hay in their barn
and ran over when I called. He went up the tree without ladder or hook or anything but his own agile body.
When he was practically out of sight, I mustered as
much of a scream as possible and begged him to come
down. I could just make out his brown face peering
through the foliage.

"Don't worry," he called. "Someone up there will
look after me."

And someone did, for he came squirreling down
with a screeching Siamese under one arm. She seemed
to have eight legs, all flailing wildly.

When Frank married and moved away, George took
over and plowed the cornfield, cut dead trees in the
upper woods, and carried out the ashes from our spectacular furnace, which was called an Iron Fireman. It
fed on bite-sized coal and blew out tons of ashes into a
huge hopper.

And then came Willie, the youngest, who was destined to be part of the family. He used to climb out of
the bedroom window and come over at night to do his
homework, partly because we had electricity and partly
because his father did not feel schooling was needed for
a farmer.

When he went in the Navy, I cried all night. Although he was never sent overseas, his naval experience
did teach him how to swim. Now he is a stocky, big,

successful foreman in a factory and lives with his wife down the road. He will get up at one or two in the morning to come over if I find "the electric" has gone out or think the furnace is going to explode. We go out to dinner fairly often and reminisce about his childhood. He likes me to go in his beloved Volvo, which is almost impossible for me to get into, but he always says happily, "Don't worry, I'll just toss you in like a sack of potatoes." Which he does.

A good many changes came about in time. The furnace is now an oil burner, and the oil is pumped into a tank through a pipe which leads from an opening below my bedroom window. The oil truck parks outside the picket fence, the oil man drags in a big hose and unlocks the cover of the inlet pipe, and the oil flows down into the cellar tank. The old cast-iron range finally rusted out, and an electric range replaced it. The electric range is a push-button affair, and the TV antenna perches on the steep roof.

And the great fireplace chimney is cleaned with a mechanical affair instead of a man who dangled heavy chains down from the roof, which of course sent soot all over the keeping room. A modern electric pump automatically pumps the water from the well, which is fed by springs.

The family changed, too. When we came to the farm, David could stand up in the great fireplace, although both girls had to bend a little. Later we measured their growth by putting pencil marks on the adjacent woodwork. We firmly believed our three were the most gifted, charming, beautiful children who ever existed—a belief which has stood the test of time.

Even during the teen-age period, we slept soundly at night, although it was difficult when all three began to look down on us and point out our shortcomings. Such remarks as "Of course, Mama, you belong in the Victorian era," or "Don't you think you could *do something* about your hair?" or "You don't really understand!" We survived, cherishing the occasional favorable comment. When we sat up at night, we repeated slight words of praise over and over.

Country living makes the stress of family living easier, for children can get away from it all by going out in the woods or down to the pond or off on their bicycles. We could also escape a stormy argument by going to the old orchard to hunt for morel mushrooms or look for arbutus. By suppertime all of us gathered peacefully by the fire while a juicy steak sizzled over the embers.

It is only now when I have seen that supposedly American family, the Louds, on television and in interviews and being written about so frequently that I realize we would have made very dull material for a series. Perhaps we were all too busy to have time to sit around an Olympic swimming pool sipping cocktails while our ears suffered through rock music. We did swim in the pond along with the eels, the fish, and the small turtles, but there never was a crisis about cleaning the pond. It is fed by two brooks that run down through the woods. At the lower end it bubbles over the rocks to the stream that flows past George's barn. The girls played recorders, and that melancholy music is not like rock in any sense. And instead of lolling in the sun, they shelled peas while David lugged in firewood for the long cool evenings.

The main impression I gained from the Louds was that they never had anything to work at or really be involved in. In any case, our own family had a sense of unity that never left us, and I shall always believe family life is the best foundation for a good society. Certainly I cannot imagine ours fitting into a commune or any kind of impersonal group living.

Anyway, our three did turn out to be everything we had dreamed of. And sometimes when I sit with friends by the open fire, which burns as brightly as it did when we moved to Stillmeadow, I realize once more how fortunate we were that day we battled the snowdrifts and found our home in the country. The ancient house speaks to us. Footfalls sound on the steep stairs, doors open softly, floorboards creak, echoing lives lived here long, long ago. And I think echoes of the lives of our family will be here too.

Meanwhile, tonight as I watch the moon in silvery mystery rising over the swamp, I speak to Stillmeadow. "Tomorrow will be fair."

WINTER

Nobody really knows when winter begins in New England. There will be mild days in November, and there will be bitter ones. Nobody knows either when Indian summers begin. Sometimes we seem to have two or three in our valley and sometimes not one. But most of us feel Indian summer comes after the killing frost. It is as if summer is looking back over her shoulder, and it is a special delight.

The leaves fall, so the dazzling color is gone, but now we see the shapes of trees and shrubs. Only the oaks keep their leaves, dark garnet in tint. Why don't they shed their leaves when every other tree does? In winter the leaves turn spice brown, but they still cling.

Practically speaking, our lives change now. We are done with salads and mousses and molded desserts. All those sandwich lunches are forgotten. We want hot Vegetable Soup or Welsh Rarebit—and sometimes Baked Stuffed Mushrooms for supper. My favorite recipe for this came from Ernest Pearson. It calls for 1 pound lean hamburg; 1 large green pepper, diced; and 1 medium onion, diced. Season with $\frac{1}{4}$ teaspoon each of salt, pepper, and powdered garlic, and ½ teaspoon Accent. Mix together and stuff large mushroom caps (about 15). Cook in a shallow casserole and add ½ ounce of sherry wine. Pour melted butter over them during the baking. Cook in a 450 degree oven about ten minutes. Serves two.

I use my favorite seasoned salt and seasoned pepper, and a little more sherry if the mushrooms are very large. Serve with a tossed salad and hot rolls. You need the large mushrooms for this dish, the bigger the better, so it is easy to stuff them and have the stuffing stay in place while they cook. Corn muffins are also good with this. If company drops in, double the recipe. You will never have a single mushroom cap left.

Recipes are a mystery to me. I have written five cookbooks, and yet I find new recipes all the time. And I cannot stop collecting them. Last week I received Alma's Orange Delight and think it delicious.

It calls for 1 cup fresh bread crumbs, 1 scant cup sugar, 1 cup milk, 3 oranges—the grated rind of one and the juice and pulp of all three, and 3 beaten eggs. Mix all the ingredients together and pour into a buttered mold or ring. Bake at 375 degrees for 45 minutes or until a silver knife, when inserted, comes out clean. Serve with whipped cream. Serves four to six. It will be juicy when you turn it out, so be careful! You may serve this warm or cold. I think it better warm.

One item on the menu is never changed at Stillmeadow, and that is the Thanksgiving turkey. We experimented with oyster stuffing and chestnut stuffing and sausage stuffing, but we like just plain stuffing best of all. However, Shirley's Sausage Stuffing pleases those who *never* eat dressing at all. This calls for 1 pound sausage meat, 1 pound ground beef, 1½ cans seasoned bread crumbs, 1 teaspoon oregano, 1 teaspoon garlic salt, 1 teaspoon salt, a dash or two of pepper, 2 tablespoons teriyaki sauce, turkey giblets boiled until tender (reserve the liquid), 4 onions, 1 green pepper, 4 stalks celery, 1 or 2 eggs.

Brown the sausage and beef in a large skillet. Place the crumbs and seasoning in a bowl. Grind the giblets, onions, green pepper, and celery, and add to the bread crumbs. Mix well. Add the browned meat. Add enough of the giblet water to moisten (add a little more warm water if necessary). Blend in the eggs, slightly beaten. Stuff the turkey, and roast until done. If your turkey is a small one, put the excess stuffing in a greased baking dish and bake in a moderate (350 degree) oven during the last hour the turkey is roasting. This is really a super stuffing. It is excellent sliced thin the next day with cold sliced turkey and cranberry sauce.

I have some close friends who insist they hate to cook. For one thing, they say, it is so dull. And whatever you make is consumed in a jiffy, and you have nothing to show for it. I think they subconsciously go back to the past when gentlewomen never opened the kitchen door. But, after all, they themselves had to eat. And the art of cooking was probably born when the first primitive woman dropped a chunk of raw meat in the embers of the fire. That smoky charred piece of meat must have been an exciting experience for the tribe.

I doubt whether anyone then bothered about equal rights. The men did the hunting, and the women took care of the quarry brought in. I feel sure most of the women were satisfied not to go charging around after wild animals but to stay in the dubious security of the camp.

Later on, in the age of chivalry, the men fought the battles, staggering around in armor, and those who lived to get home consumed vast quantities of food, if the reports are true. I can imagine an early conversation when the husband doffed his helmet and sank down, saying, "Haven't we got anything decent to eat?"

"If you spent more time hunting and less fighting, we would have."

Just when the era of helpless woman began, I do not know, but there are remnants of it even today. When a woman says, "I can't even boil an egg," she echoes the bygone days. She is also talking nonsense. She may never be a gourmet cook, but if she can read, she can follow directions in a cookbook and turn out a passable meal. And my observation is that a really superb meal is remembered and thus provides extra pleasure.

With electric ranges (often with self-cleaning ovens) and electric dishwashers, not to mention toasters and electric coffeemakers and beaters, today's homemaker has plenty of cooking aids. With the help of electric freezers, meals may be made ahead and tucked away. Even if a home has no freezer, the freezing compartment in the refrigerator will store a great deal, and the new freezer bags make storage easier.

It helps, I find, to plan ahead and to keep a list of what is in the freezer. Otherwise, it is possible to come home late after a meeting and open the freezer and find nothing except frozen Harvard beets. Good as they are, you need something to go with them.

As I think about modern cooking, I believe the

most common error is overcooking. Even an elegant
roast beef can be dry and tough if overcooked, and lamb
loses its flavor. Vegetables get mushy, custards curdle,
and so on. Eggs are very sensitive; they easily become
leathery. They should be brought to room temperature
before cooking whether they are to be boiled, fried,
baked, or used in an omelet. For top-of-the-stove cooking, a heavy skillet or pan is best—my favorite is an old
cast-iron frying pan. For baked eggs, individual ceramic
casseroles are useful. Egg poachers are available in most
stores that carry housewares, but an egg poached in boiling water in a small skillet is excellent, especially if you
add a little vinegar to the cooking water. When you cook
eggs, it is better not to go in the next room but to stay
right by the stove. A long telephone conversation can
ruin the best of eggs.

During one of the shortage periods in the Depression, we bought thirteen hens and established them in
an unused kennel with a good fenced-in run. It was exciting to go out with a basket and gather the eggs and
have really fresh eggs to cook. The one problem (and a
big one) was that the hens all began to be personal
friends. The original idea was that when they stopped
being layers, we would have them killed and stock the
freezer with fine roasting chickens. But we were not able
to face it.

"If you think I could possibly eat one of those nice
hens, you are crazy," I said. So in the end we gave them
away and went on buying chicken at the market.

One fine feature of our life with the hens was that
we had so many eggs we were able to put some down in
water glass in a big stoneware crock. I do not know

whether anyone does this now. The water glass was a liquid, and the eggs were gently submerged in it. The theory was that this sealed the eggs, and it certainly worked. It was a pleasant feeling on a January day to know we had a whole crockful of eggs, and we missed it when the hens were gone.

Our hens laid large brown eggs, and the yolks were golden yellow. The only time white eggs are desirable, we have always felt, is at Easter, for they do take Easter-egg coloring better than the brown. Most shoppers, I notice, want white eggs whose yolks are pale, and it is increasingly difficult to buy brown eggs. Also the eggs labeled "X large" are nowhere near the size of our eggs. Our hens would hardly consider them eggs at all.

One of my favorite egg dishes is Daisy Eggs. Use one egg to a person and separate the yolks from the whites, keeping each yolk in an individual dish. Beat the whites until stiff and add seasoned salt and seasoned pepper and a dash of Worcestershire sauce. Spoon the beaten egg whites into flat greased ramekins, or pile them in individual mounds on a greased baking sheet. Now slip a yolk onto each white and bake in a moderate oven (325 degrees) until the yolks are set and the whites begin to brown. Serve at once. For a holiday brunch serve with popovers or corn muffins or toast rounds. Some guests will want two Daisy Eggs to keep that hungry wolf from the door. We like this for breakfast on New Year's Day.

Another favorite is Caracas Eggs. The recipe was given me by my beloved English professor at college. It calls for 4 ounces shredded dried beef, 2 tablespoons butter, 1 teaspoon chili powder, ½ pound grated Ameri-

can cheese, 2 cups stewed tomatoes, 6 beaten eggs, seasoned salt and pepper to taste. Place the beef in a heavy skillet with the butter, chili powder, cheese, and tomatoes. Cook over low heat until the mixture bubbles. Add the eggs and continue stirring until it thickens. Serve on thin slices of buttered toast. This serves four to six, and makes an elegant lunch with tossed salad. I often use canned stewed tomatoes when I am in a hurry.

There is a strangeness about a winter morning when the temperature is zero or below. Day begins with a pale glimmer along the horizon beyond the lacings of dark branches. The trees in this New England valley are famous for their brilliant autumn coloring but in winter are spectacular without the masking of foliage. The giant sugar maples all around Stillmeadow lift a circular pattern to the light, the lower branches like spread fans and every twig curved with grace. The old apple orchard has an occasional tree left, and apple trees branch out close to the ground, and the limbs twist irregularly. With snow outlining them in white velvet, they need no drift of apple blossoms to be lovely.

The junipers and white pines at the swamp's edge seem dark and thick in contrast and at the early hours quiver with winter birds. The willows by the pond are like stilled fountains and seem to give forth light. The rusty garnet of oak is not visible from my windows, but it isn't far to Great Oak Road. Alas, our black-walnut trees died, and only one butternut is left at the edge of Jeremy Swamp Road, a massive heritage from long ago. But it stands in bare splendor as the light deepens. Now thickets by the swamp take on color—all shades of brown.

The sky is pale, but the snow is like the inside of a shell. A scientist could explain it—I only wonder at it.

As I open the upper half of the Dutch door, the cold air slices in and whips against the warm, dense air of the house. The keeping room smells of wood smoke from last night's fire and of my white-lilac cologne and of apples and oranges and grapes in the wooden fruit bowl by the hearth. It may also smell of Stillmeadow Beef Stew, which simmered half the night in the old Dutch oven. But I am only half-conscious of this until the absolute clarity and purity of the outside air come in. I breathe deeply and feel as if I had pools of ice in my lungs, but keep the door open so I can listen to the silence.

There are many silences—so many I would like to write a book about them, beginning with the first pulsing silence after the words "I love you . . ." to the heavy quiet after a tragic piece of news.

There is the stillness of a summer noon and the quiet of ebb tide. But I think perhaps the winter-morning stillness has the most magic. Quite literally there is no sound. And therefore the motionless air seems to sing —a melody from the beginning of time. I cannot analyze it, but my heart also stands still. Of course this singing silence is rare, for winter has a whole orchestra of her own, and the sounds of winter are chiefly percussion notes—the crack of ice, the plop of snowfall from the roof, the crash as a tree gives up a branch under the weight of snow. The harsh cries of bluejays and the call of an owl at night and occasionally the scream of a bobcat in the upper woods all announce that it is January. Then there is the snowplow lumbering down the road

and Adams's oil truck braking outside the picket fence
(a lovely sound, that is).

We live in a world of noise and confusion, and a
good many scientists agree that man suffers from it. We
are bombarded with noise from jet planes to riveting
machines, from subways to sirens. And I think, as I feel
the healing of the winter-morning stillness, that we all
desperately need some quietude in our lives. I notice
how we scream at parties and shout at meetings and
what a tendency the young have to toss bombs and
smash windows, and I wonder whether part of this isn't
a reaction to frayed nerves.

In any case, as I go about the business of adding my
own noise to the day, while the coffeepot bubbles and
bacon sizzles and the toaster pops up, I feel I can face the
day because I have been restored. The pipes may freeze;
the furnace may go off; all the usual stresses of midwinter must be met. But I carry the magic of early morning
on a still day and am grateful.

Winter means work; there is no arguing around
that. Nature does not make it easy. Snow shoveling,
plowing the road, thawing the car out, getting in firewood, cleaning the ashes from the hearth, filling the bird
feeders—and always and forever mopping up melted
snow, thawing frozen pipes, feeding stray barn cats—all
of this would be alien to a tropical inhabitant. But mankind, whatever else one may say, has the ability to adapt
and manage, whatever the climate involves.

Successful living, I suspect, depends on how will-
ingly we do adapt to the environment. New Englanders
adapt, which is one reason life here is so pleasant. When
it is 20 or 30 degrees below zero, Art Olsen, the plumber,

may come at night to get the furnace going again. His boots will have a glaze of ice from the preceding emergency call. His face is ruddy with cold, making his sea-blue eyes startlingly intense.

"How dreadful to have to come out on such a night," I may say.

The typical Yankee answer comes firmly: "We got to expect it this time of year." Or sometimes, "Well, I don't care for the tropics myself. Too hot, too many bugs." Or "This snow is good for the ground. Nature knows what it's all about." Or "We take what we get. Spring's coming in time."

I am especially impressed by the girls at the village beauty shop. Time is what they sell, as well as skill. On a day when the roads are impassable, they—at least some of them—manage to walk to the beauty shop, and then the cancellations come in. I have never heard a word of complaint. It's just the way it is.

I find that I feel apologetic if I complain about the weather, and only go so far as to say mildly that I have been housebound for over a week and am glad to get out. The typical Yankee answer to this, quite properly, is that I have been warm and cozy, and since I work at home, I could just spend more time at the typewriter.

As I have known many people through the years in this valley, I feel there is a strength in most Americans that sometimes is clouded over in the violence of the times. It is there. I think it will always be there. It is not limited to New England, as I was reminded when my dear friend Dallas in California wrote that one of those disastrous fires had burned her house to the ground. But she was lucky, she wrote, for she saved both of the miniature poodles—she grabbed their leashes as the flames came near, hooked the ends over the door while she scooped up her purse, and got out. Dallas Burnette is the widow of Smiley Burnette, the long-time Hollywood actor, who was a dearly loved friend. Their first experience in New England was when they came to visit us, and it was an alien world—dark, wooded, hilly. Queer old houses with small-paned windows. No fireplaces in the middle of a glassed-in room with curved hoods to catch the smoke.

So, in many ways, we were worlds apart. But when Dallas wrote about the fire that swept over the whole community and finished the letter by saying, "Of course, a good many priceless papers that were Smiley's and some personal things were destroyed as well as the home and all the furnishings, but wasn't it lucky I could get the dogs out—and my car was burning, but a man came by just in time to get us in his and we got to the top of the hill. I am so thankful!" I then felt the basic strength of the people in our whole country more than I ever had. I remembered tornado victims, flood victims, hurricane victims in past years who seemed able to pick up and go on, just because they always had. I am glad that with all the disastrous events going on, I can find that I have faith in my country because of this single quality, if for no other reason.

And all these thoughts were initiated by my philosophizing about the New England cheerfulness in January and February. But Dallas, out in the California desert country, is much like a neighbor down the road who risked his life pulling some children out of an ice-deep lake they had fallen into. This quality I so revere is not localized.

However, some characteristics are indigenous to a

region as some trees are—and I look out at the great
stark maples on Jeremy Swamp Road and somehow feel
they describe the New England personality. They have
a rugged grandeur. They are not breathtaking like the
redwoods or dramatic like palms, and they do not have
the lyric beauty of a white-birch woods such as I grew
up with in Wisconsin, but they are there as the blizzards
beat down, and the new life of spring is tight in their leaf
buds. The miracle of growth is in them, and on a winter
morning I watch the light of a new day being born and
their countless twigs glowing with it.

As the birds come in, there is sound in the winter
morning. There is nothing like my song sparrow on
Cape Cod in summer, who begins at 4:00 A.M. and is
still singing at nine at night. The general and sometimes
feverish chorus of bird song diminishes toward the end
of summer. But there are twitters and chirps and clicks
and blue-jay assertions in winter. There is the sound of
scrabbling as a bevy of birds tries to take over the feeder.
And the silence is ended.

I notice the house sounds are different in winter,
for the old house has her own language. The ancient
wide floor boards creak, the furnace rumbles into action,
and the hot-water radiators make a bubbling sound. The
fire in the great fireplace talks all day. There is a special
sound when the last log breaks and falls into embers
around midnight. Then, too, people who come in arrive
stamping their boots, shaking their mittens, and saying,
"Wow!" or "Whooo!" The cold comes in with them, as
definite as an extra layer of clothing. I always feel like
saying, "Take off the cold and dump it in the fireplace."

Voices change, too. To me, they seem to have an

added firmness, as if the whole person were pulled together more tightly. It is difficult to describe the tone quality, but I believe I could identify the season by hearing people's voices. At 10 or 20 below, I myself speak softly, conserving what energy I have.

Like any generalization, this has no universal application, for a Christmas eggnog party is far from quiet. Everyone is happy to be together and to exchange dramatic tales of frozen pipes, cracked windowpanes, stalled motors. The sharing transforms all the trials into adventures, and suddenly they seem rather gay. At Stillmeadow, too, nobody will stay in the comfortable front parlor, because the great hearth in the keeping room is a magnet. Guests prefer to stand all evening, just to be near the beautiful fire. To what David Frost calls the festivities is added the plain common-garden pleasure of being together, for in winter we do not see one another often.

It reminds me of the time Connie called up from New York to see how I survived the latest and worst blizzard.

"I had a wonderful time," I told her. "Today was wonderful, that is what it was."

"You got out to the market," she said.

"Yes, and I had a visit with George and Joe and Peggy and some neighbors. It was a perfect day!"

The cold came suddenly this month like a great wave rolling in from some limitless frozen tundra. Sunset shone like a knife blade, and all the birds vanished. The squirrels tore the bird feeder from the maple, gobbling a last life-sustaining meal, and then they too were gone. The barn cats I feed came for warm milk and buried their noses in the pan by the well house. A cat normally eats daintily, pausing to wash her face, but all I could see from the kitchen window were the humped-up rears and stiff tails as the cats gobbled. Then their paw marks dotted the snow as they made for the shelter of the barn across the road.

The furnace began to breathe thickly like an asthmatic man in a commercial for magic pills. In reasonable weather she purrs; now she panted. By the time supper was over, it was zero. The next time I looked, it was 5 below. What the weathermen so cheerily call the wind chill made the back kitchen (which is always cold) feel like Fairbanks, Alaska. We have electric light cords plugged in under the sink and beside the back-toilet pipes. The 60-watt bulbs attached to them help to prevent the water pipes from freezing under ordinary conditions. I turned them on and opened one sink faucet slightly so it would drip. I put extra logs on the fire and stuffed a bath towel in the window sill by my bed where the cold air works its way in, despite the storm sash. Then I faced the perpetual problem: whether to leave faucets dripping and take a chance that the well would not go dry, or turn them off and just pray.

By midnight it was 10 below zero and at four in the morning 20 below. I turned up the unwilling furnace. The drains in both kitchens and the shower off the back kitchen were already frozen. One faucet in the middle kitchen worked, so I filled all the buckets and pitchers and pans I could find. Then I listened to weather reports until five and decided to go to sleep since there was nothing else to do.

Heating an ancient house is never easy, but Still-meadow is rather special. My bedroom, workroom, TV room, and reading room combined is right over the furnace, and one wall is against the great central chimney around which the house was built. So this room is tropical when the furnace is turned up. The keeping room, which is next to it, has five doors and two outside walls and cools off rapidly. From thence one goes to the middle kitchen (there is no front kitchen), which is like a refrigerator. There is no cellar under either kitchen (just a crawlway rather open to the outside air).

Stepping into the back kitchen when it is 20 below outside takes courage, since that room is *all* windows, outside walls, and a door. The shower mat freezes solid to the floor. The air ices toward you even with the enormous hot-water radiator bubbling away and a wall heater going. The toilet bowl utters a last desperate gurgle and gives up.

During one of these spells, I keep the fireplace going day and night so some heat sifts into that frigid back kitchen. My son-in-law spends weekends cutting more wood, but always wondering where last week's woodshedful has gone. What did I *do* with all that wood?

Art Olsen comes then with his excellent crew, and the cellar is full of conversation as they thaw out pipes, stop leaks, battle the drains. When the dishwasher motor cracked open, it was like saying good-bye to a dear old friend. It was put in in 1945, as my date-minded friend Alice Blinn reminded me. They do not make them like it any more. I wanted to write a poem of farewell but was kept too busy carrying dishwater to throw out the back door.

This old dishwasher operated by turning one switch. It minded its own business, and everything came out shining clean. The modern dishwasher I have at the Cape has so many cycles and so many buttons that it is as complicated as a moon launching. I find all appliances of today are overcomplex for me and therefore frequently out of order. I suppose the manufacturers feel they must always have something new as a selling point. But I think they are mistaken about the average homemaker, who likes things easy to manage.

There is one thing I have not read in comments on the rigors of winter. The special triumph when pipes are thawed, the furnace purrs along, the car is shoveled out—these make life suddenly glow. When my shower works once more, what a treat a hot shower is! Rupert Brooke called it the benison of hot water. The miracle of hot water coming from the kitchen faucet is hard to overestimate. The wonder of lights going on, after the power has been off, never grows dim. So many things we take for granted are really blessings.

I often think a stranger coming to my frozen valley in midwinter would find a quality in people he might not have experienced elsewhere. After thirty-eight or so years, I am still awed by the quality I can only describe as built-in kindness. For instance, when Art and his men have worked day and night and look shaggy and worn, they do not need any extra activity. But one night after they had worked in the cellar all day, up and down the ladder-steep stairs, out to the truck and back, the cellar door was left ajar. Instantly my Abyssinian slid down to the mysterious depths. I called and called, being unable to negotiate the steps, but for once she was deaf. The next thing I knew, a tall, dark young man came bounding into the keeping room with a small kitten dangling under one arm.

"Thought I better bring Amber up," said Bob, "so you wouldn't worry." Incidentally, Amber, who does not cotton to strangers as my mother would say, was not hissing or clawing. She let her front legs fall limp on his oil-soaked jacket. Bob handed her over and toiled back to the lower depths.

Certainly my wandering kitten was no concern of his, and he had troubles enough since the pipes would *not* thaw that time. The lovely quality of kindness simply bubbled up in him.

And once I decided to try to cross the ice from the house to the car one below-zero day. Whether I was foolish or courageous is open to question, for if I fell, nobody would have known it for several hours. When I skidded along with my cane, I saw an unfamiliar thickset woman walking down the road. Since nobody ever walks down the road except Erwin or his sister, I stared in disbelief. I had never seen her before or the small boy rabbiting along beside her.

She stopped and then opened the gate for me, held out a firm arm, opened the car door, and waited until I was safely inside. I never did learn her name. But as she went on up the hill, vanishing into mystery, I felt a glow of satisfaction knowing that kindness is so tangible in this valley.

Another day I went to the post office. My mail had to go out, and I put a rubber band around it and got to the shopping center before I realized it would be impossible to get up or down the icy post office steps. Just then a woman started up the steps, and I leaned out of the car and said timidly, "Would you mind putting this in with yours?"

"Not at all," she said briskly. And then while I was starting the motor, she came skidding back across the ice. "I brought your rubber band," she said. "They always come in handy." I shall never know her name, either.

One day a man came to saw up a load of wood my dear neighbor Willie had brought. It was factory two-by-fours, hard wood, which Willie had stacked by the gate. I located Bill Lewis in the village directory, because he has a chain saw. He came on the day that week it stopped snowing. It was, again, below zero.

"May as well split some of those big logs out back," he said, "and put them in your woodshed. Going to be cold tonight. Some of them are too big for you to carry."

This did not add a penny to his fee. It was just kindness.

I could multiply these by a hundred instances during this one winter. The loving thoughtfulness of friends is in a different category but equally precious. Jean and Oscar Lovdal have a farm down the road and work as hard and long as farmers must. But there is never a day during a bad cold spell when the phone does not ring and I hear Jean's warm, ebullient voice.

"Is your furnace going? How are your pipes? I'll run over with a baked chicken breast for your supper. I know you won't want to go out."

Or, "Have you enough firewood to keep the fire going all night?"

Or, "Can I do any errands for you?"

Or, "Just thought I'd ring up and see if you are all right."

When I get to the market, George and Joe Tomey tell me if I run out of anything just give them a ring and they'll bring it out. (They do not deliver in this scattered area.) Even if I need a loaf of bread, it's no problem to drop it off on their way home (which is seven or eight miles away).

And then there is Livvy at the village beauty shop.

"If you can't get out," she says in her soft, dark voice, "I'll come over at night and give you a shampoo any time."

She lives on Poverty Road, which is a long haul, and she has had severe foot trouble from long hours of standing. She also has her house to run and her family to feed. But all I need to do is call her, she says, and gives me her home phone number.

In this troubled and fiercely aggressive period, I find the natural kindness of the folk in this rural area constantly renews my faith in humanity. The riots and bombs and screaming mobs are a reality we have to face. But there are basic qualities in human beings which are *not* destroyed, and this comforts and sustains me when I hear someone on television who says we must destroy-destroy-destroy.

I also believe if we followed the simple direction "Be ye kind one to another" and extended it to mean nations as well as peoples, the cancer of war would be wiped out once and for all. Imagine a world in which, instead of dropping bombs on alien villages, we spent the price of one bomb on food to drop instead. Suppose, instead of counting success by how many young enemies we killed in a week, we tossed clothing and medicines over the bloody front lines. I admit I am a natural idealist, but why not try this? It wouldn't cost much, as costs go.

Very few people any longer believe that wars can be won. More than 46,000 young men have been killed in the extravagant folly of Vietnam. Among them were unknown numbers whose energy would have brought new strength to this tired planet. Their talents and potentialities should not end in a grave, or a hospital. And how can we believe we are the most civilized nation in the world after killing more people than any other nation in history?

There are so many objectives man's aggressiveness could turn to—hunger, disease, the rapidly rotting planet herself.

By December in the valley, we are ready for the long cold, and there is excitement in the air as we wait for the first snowstorm. At the market we quote the *Farmer's Almanac*, which is our constant companion, and we are pleased it promises a white Christmas. Meanwhile, we are busy stocking those emergency shelves, filling the woodshed with logs, checking the snow tires, bringing in greens for the mantels. Some of the ancient houses are already banked around the foundations with evergreen branches to keep out the cold.

Alice and Anne, the grandchildren, gather fallen dead branches and twigs for kindling and help their father clean out the birdhouses for one more time (they make a nice shelter for the winter birds). The bird feeders are filled to spilling point, and there is suet in the cage on one maple. The girls bring the little rubber boat from the pond, now quiet and dark with fallen leaves. Then they hopefully hunt for the sleds and metal slider and the skates (there is always one missing).

Their father decides we need more wood, although the woodpile is window-sill high by the back door, so he vanishes into the old orchard and saws more dead limbs and drags them in.

"Might run short," he puffs.

Connie and I make trips to Woodbury for more boots for everyone and end by buying some "adorable" sweaters at Deschino's. I can never, never resist a sweater. Both grandchildren have outgrown last year's storm jackets. Now they are thirteen and eleven and, as any mother will agree, they are never the same size long enough to wear anything out.

We take a couple of weekends off when the rest of the family drives in from New York and New Jersey. Our theme song is, "Come while the roads are still open."

Like all houses built in 1690, Stillmeadow has small rooms, but there are a good many of them, and to Jill and me the house seemed commodious. When Jill died, the children had their own homes in various places, but the ancient homestead is still the center for the family, although I get a little dizzy adding us up, for I always come out with fourteen.

Five of the grandchildren have really outgrown sleeping bags, but there is always room around the great fireplace and at the harvest table Jill built. And Connie and Barbara always manage to provide elegant casseroles, salads, hot rolls, and desserts. All of them arrive with cars full of food. It all belongs with the holiday month.

Then there comes a day without wind and with a flat sky the color of pewter. Amber, my Abyssinian kitten, sits on the window sill overlooking the swamp, and when the first big spangles of snow fall against the old bubbly-glass panes, she switches her tail wildly and tries to catch them, although she really knows they are outside. The flakes fall casually, circling in the darkening air, but by midnight the yard is spread with lace, the swamp crested with foam. Inside, the ancient floors begin to creak with the cold, and I like to imagine the ghosts of long-gone folk walking about, just checking to be sure everything is snug.

In the morning there is a new world outside, pure and dazzling, and I hear my son-in-law say, "I can't find the snow shovels. Who put them away?"

Usually the first big snow melts, because the earth still has some late warmth in it and a little softness, but I've never known a man to put off shoveling snow. It is a kind of special triumph.

Jill planted a stand of Christmas trees when we first came, but as they grew, we found we never could cut a single one. We took our trees from the woods up the hill, where thinning was needed. Other people drove down Jeremy Swamp Road at night and cut what they wanted, but some are still left, tall and beautiful, a beginning of more forested land. Once you have planted and nourished a tree, it is hard to cut it down. The last few years, we have bought our tree, presumably from a tree farm in Maine, and I go over with Erwin, my neighbor boy, to bring it back. I confess the sight of the great stacks of trees makes me sad, although Erwin points out that they are already cut down, so why worry? I think we shall see the day when any tree must wear a certificate saying it really is from a tree farm and not a natural forest.

I do not like artificial trees, however. The symbolism of the evergreen is of life and growth, as are holly and Christmas greens. I am apt to go around singing "Deck the halls with boughs of holly" as the tree goes into its metal stand, and I like to think we are following a tradition of centuries past as we light the candles on Christmas Eve and sit by the fire singing carols, supplementing them with Christmas music on the stereo (a concession to modern times).

Our tree has ornaments saved for years, and the glass star goes on the tip, although it has lost quite a few points by now. The children all have favorites, and if one little carved animal from Germany is missing, it *must* be found. Amber has a desire to climb the branches and knock off something shiny and has to be persuaded to chase her own traditional toy, which is a tiny woolen wreath she can carry in her small mouth.

The Christmas tree lights go outside and not on the tree. All along the valley Christmas lights are strung on trees and bushes, and it is a happy sight to drive to Woodbury at dusk-dark and see the glow. Every house has lighted front windows, too, and the village centers are decorated with crèches, stars, huge electric candles, and garlanded store windows.

The gifts pile up under the tree, and there is much secret wrapping and many admonitions not to open this or that door. The new soft woolen ties are lovely and easy to manage—I am the world's most incompetent wrapper of gifts. But there is a problem with Amber, who loves to grab one end of a tie and swallow it. We spend some time hauling lavender and rose and green yarn out of her mouth.

Gift time is a delight, but I feel the most important

part of Christmas has nothing to do with material things. It is a matter of the heart, of thinking about those we love and cherishing the happy times we have had together. And it is a time to stop counting up everything wrong with the world and consider what we have that is good, and to hope that in some way we may help bring more joy to this small piece of the planet we inhabit.

Most of all it is time to remember the Baby whose birth we celebrate and to wonder all over again how this humble Child has affected the world more than all the powerful men who have ever lived. His simple words "Thou shalt love thy neighbour as thyself" would yet save mankind if we followed them.

When Stillmeadow finally quiets down on Christmas Eve and the fire in the great hearth burns to embers and the candles are snuffed, I go outside to be sure there is enough food by the old well house for the stray cats we feed and the skunks and the coons. A last helping of warm milk is always acceptable on a cold night. The country stillness is gentle to the ear and only emphasized by the cry of one owl down by the pond or the creaking of a bough on one of the giant maples that guard the house. The bright moon casts shadows on the snow, and the stars prick the midnight sky with their infinite pattern.

And I say good night to the world as I have for many Christmas Eves.

"God rest you merry, gentlemen."

The January thaw comes unexpectedly, sudden as light after a black thunderstorm. The metallic air softens to velvet smoothness, snow shadows are overlaid with a pink tinge, the tracery of sky-reaching branches is not black but gentler charcoal. The snowy meadow herself loses the rigid sparkle of intense cold and mellows to ermine. The sky is like a blue lagoon. And when I wake in the morning and hear the plop of icicles melting on the old well-house roof, I think it the sweetest music on earth.

Icicles are beautiful, and my granddaughter Anne often tries to bring a three-foot one into the house. One of the disappointments of childhood is to find that a warm kitchen turns a shining spear of ice to a wet spot on the floor. The wisteria that climbs the well house is lacy with icicles most of the winter, but the enormous ones depend from the roof. When the melt begins, they fall with a tinkle like broken glass.

If the thaw persists a few days, there comes the crackling music of the brook as bits of ice pile up against the stony barrier by George's barn. The Black Angus in his barn feel the atmospheric change and bellow in their throaty, thick voices. The birds at the feeder add a conversation to the sunny air.

At the market people sound gay, and I notice in the parking lot they move more loosely, not scrunched up and bent against the dreadful chill. We talk of an early end to winter and report the lilac buds are truly swelling (lilac buds are nature's optimists).

My beloved New Jersey friends, Helen, Vicky, and Olive, suddenly feel like coming for a weekend and enjoy what I call a glut of hiking. They hike before breakfast in the dense woods up the hill. They take a brief walk after lunch down Jeremy Swamp Road, and around midnight decide to take a look at the meadow in moonlight. There is still time enough for cheese fondue or Stillmeadow Beef Stew and, later, popcorn exploding into fluffy whiteness in the long-handled corn popper Helen holds carefully over the embers in the open fire.

The thaw is nature's promise, sometimes brief as the life of an open rose, and occasionally lasting a week. But how exciting! Erwin, my teen-ager from down the road, describes it in a word. "Gorgeous!" he says as he brings in more wood. "Gorgeous!"

Now I try to do all the errands that have piled up when I was housebound. The cheese shop in Woodbury is the first stop. It smells delicious, with a mingling of cheese odors. There are more cheeses than I can count, as well as herbs and spices and imported mustards and sweetmeats and crisp English crackers. Then there are brown-pottery-covered soup bowls, French crèpe pans, turquoise and tangerine cast-iron enamel-covered skillets, cheese boards. I always come out with enough assorted cheese to last a month and just a couple of those cooking utensils I cannot resist and do not need. Mr. and Mrs. Alogna, who own the cheese shop, are warm and friendly and keep a bowl of tidbits by the counter. I have spent a good deal of time in cheese shops in various parts of the country, and in only one have I found the proprietor as cold as a refrigerator. So I believe living with delectable cheeses tends to make a person interested in good living and good conversation.

My second stop during the thaw is the Woodbury flower shop. As I walk into the greenhouse, the exuberance of nature is tangible. The air smells of damp, rich soil and moist plant leaves. The warmth could be gathered up in my hand. There is an indoor fountain there, and the murmur of falling water adds to the sensation that I have strayed into a semitropical haven. If I splurge and buy my favorite yellow roses, I always find an extra rose tucked in. When I buy practically, I choose half a dozen pink carnations. Their spicy odor is lovely and the cool texture of their petals gentle to touch. I put them in the moss-rose teapot that has been in the family since time began, and the keeping room has a garden sweetness by the time the wall of cold moves in again.

At the market, Erwin and I buy two carloads of supplies, and I spend a lot of extra time just visiting. Often, before he has the car unloaded, a pencil of chill wind writes the end of the thaw, and by nightfall the thermometer plunges down as fast as a waterfall.

But the promise of the thaw stays in memory like the echo of a melody. February brings the final signature of winter, and we then begin the climb toward spring.

On one of the days after winter had dozed off briefly, Erwin and I went to the village as usual to stock up with supplies. I think we live by the weather in New England more than people do in most places. We often forget what day of the week it is but never what the barometer reads. This day the sun was warm, and we did not hurry, so it was after four when we drove home.

When we stopped by the picket fence, we had a surprise. The yard was full of huge Black Angus cattle. Wherever there was a bare spot, they were chewing away at the stubble. The biggest one was leaning against the well house, with his mouth full.

I can never reach verbal heights in a crisis, so all I said was, "Oh, my."

Erwin was busy counting the Angus and got up to thirteen.

"Well," he said shakily. "I don't mind any of them except that one with horns."

"They got out of George's barn," I said, "but how did they get through the fence?"

"Must be a gate open."

"I'll go first and talk to them," I decided, "and take their minds off while you unload the car."

Erwin was not exactly fired with enthusiasm but, at sixteen, he was one I would always want beside me in trouble. He was already heaving out a fifty-pound sack of bird feed.

Trying to appear at ease, I began to visit with the guests, hoping the well house would not collapse with five or six hundred pounds of ebony from the one leaning on the supports. I had time to realize the vastness of the steers and appreciate the lush barn smell. They were too busy scrubbing up dead grass to listen to me. Only the horned one looked up and shook a tentative tail. Erwin looked very small as he tiptoed to the back-kitchen door. He had felt the fewer trips back and forth the better, so he looked like a walking load of merchandise with feet and only one eye visible. He made record speed past the well house. The path narrows there, and I almost felt the steer's steamy breath on Erwin's mound of packages.

Once inside, Erwin gulped his hot cocoa instead of gently sipping it.

"They can't stay there all night," I said. "It's going

down to zero. And the poor lonely things are having such a wonderful free time."

"Yeah," said Erwin. He is used to my feeling about caged creatures. But he was not happy. Nor was Amber, who stood saucer-eyed at the kitchen window, tail swelled three times its normal size. Her chin quivered; her ears shook.

"I guess I got to feed the birds anyway," Erwin commented.

"Wait till I try to reach George."

George was not home from work, but his wife answered. When I told her my yard was full of Black Angus, her comment was brief: "Oh, good God!"

By the time she located George and he arrived, it was dark and Erwin had turned on the yard lights to do the outside chores. George herded the steers back to the barn. I sat by the fire filled with sympathy for the poor creatures now shut up in the closeness of the barn after their brief encounter with freedom. I remembered a kind of wistful look in their great liquid eyes and the eagerness with which they pawed up what was once a lawn.

Most of us, I thought, are caged in some way all our lives. There are walls and bars and fences of all kinds, invisible but tangible. We spend a great deal of time climbing over obstacles—perhaps this is what life is all about. But we must all, I think, long for a brief time of real freedom outside the restrictions of our existence. A time, for instance, when we would toss all the clocks out of the window, take the telephone off the hook, let the doorbell ring all by itself.

Most of living is regimentation, and I was glad the

Black Angus had escaped for a few hours of delicious liberty. I hoped it would stay in their dreams.

When I said all this to Erwin, he gave me a solemn look out of his blue eyes. His reaction was simple.

"If it snows tomorrow, there won't be any school."

For to him, right now, a day of shoveling snow and lugging firewood is his idea of freedom.

On a night of falling snow and silent meadow, I take my tray to my room with a supper of lamb chops, creamed spinach, tossed salad made from the usual discouraged winter lettuce, pale tomatoes, and lacquered cucumbers. I don't know what they put on the cucumbers, by the way, to make them so slippery and shiny.

While I cut up the best of the chop meat for Amber, who sits on the desk waiting, I listen to Julia Child. By the time her hour is over, I am exhausted just watching her dice and slice and knead and roll and throw things around in a kind of Olympian abandon. Julia is the most vigorous cook I have ever observed. But I notice a good many of the delicious dishes she serves at the end of the program are taken from the oven where they are sitting—all done! I figure it would take me all day to create one of her simple little dinners, and then I would be ready to lie down and rest my aching arms.

The only thing we have in common is that both of us have written cookbooks—but my one time-consuming recipe is Stillmeadow All Day Stew, and that does not mean I spend all day in the kitchen. It means that, every now and then, I go out and toss something else in as the Dutch oven sends forth its savory smells.

My Dutch oven is my best friend, as it was my

mother's. It is black cast iron, very heavy, and works a special magic on anything put in it. It is easy to take care of, too. It won't go in the dishwasher but washes clean with warm suds and no scraping or scouring. Occasionally I season it by rubbing unsalted oil on the inside and outside, and setting it in a 250 degree oven for a short time, then wiping it clean with paper towels. This keeps it from rusting and gives it a nice shine.

The children want Beef Stew every weekend when they come out from the city. To make it I use the best beef, cut in 1½-inch (or smaller) cubes. I put flour, salt, pepper, and dried onion flakes in a bag, and shake the pieces of meat in it. In the Dutch oven I put half oil and half butter and brown the meat. Then I add marrow bones and pour a can of condensed undiluted beef consommé or bouillon over. I clap the cover on, turn the stove to low, and go about whatever other business is at hand. In about an hour, I add more liquid, which may be anything from tomato juice or vegetable juice to juice from canned mushrooms and canned peas or beans.

Then I add a cup or so of carrots cut in pieces, quartered onions or small white ones, half a parsnip, and, if I have it, a wedge or so of turnip. On my next trip through the kitchen, I add some celery and quartered potatoes. By now, if the stock is too rich, I add enough boiling water to cover, and turn the heat to simmer.

When I get around to it, I add some tomato paste and a couple of spoonfuls of good canned tomatoes, along with some mushrooms. An hour before suppertime, I let it rest to develop the flavor. Most stews and soups are benefited by a rest period (as we all are).

Connie comments, "But, Mama, it never is the same two times running."

And this is certainly true. For I may add half a cup of red canned kidney beans with the liquor, some peas, some string beans, a few ripe pitted olives, and several cut-up sausage links or slivered ham. Or a small can of corn niblets. Diced fresh parsley adds much, but dried will do, and I always like a handful of pasta—macaroni shells or noodles.

After it has bubbled long enough for the pasta to be tender but not mushy, the stew is ready to serve. We carry the Dutch oven to the trestle table and set it on a very thick steak board, remove the cover, and put the antique silver soup ladle in for dipping.

Hot garlic French bread, just right for dunking, completes the meal. We serve the stew in the old onion-pattern blue soup plates. A red wine goes well with it. For dessert fresh fruit is best, with a potful of black coffee.

I forgot to mention that slivers of fresh cabbage make a fine addition to the stew. And I use the seasoned salt and seasoned pepper.

As to amounts, by the time the stew is done it brims the Dutch oven, but there is never any left, even if only three or four of us turn up. I try to save a few tablespoonfuls for the country cats we feed because they love it, and Amber has her dish with the best pieces of beef. The marrow bones go out under the bird feeder, for the birds love the bits of gristle that cling to them.

This recipe would horrify Julia Child, since no measuring cup or spoon ever approaches it.

❈   ❈   ❈

On a winter day I like to think of the summer we spent two weeks on Cape Cod with my cousin and his wife. It was the first vacation in more years than we could count. I did not even take my typewriter. We stayed in a primitive shabby cottage with all the discomforts a house can have, including an ancient sea chest lined with zinc in which we kept big chunks of ice to serve as a refrigerator. The oil lamps were small and smoked even with new wicks. The yard was thick with poison ivy. The beds were so bad that my cousin spent half of each night sitting in a wicker rocker. We cooked on a rusty old oil stove.

But the ocean was there and the marshes and sand dunes, and sea gulls flew over all day long. Wild, deep-pink roses bloomed extravagantly. The day before we left, Rob cooked a ten-pound lobster over a fire in the back yard in a huge kettle we found.

Jill went off the next morning and came back in time for a lobster sandwich. She spoke casually. "I have bought us a piece of land on Mill Pond around the corner."

"You can't mean it!"

"We'll be coming back," she said, "and we're going to be comfortable."

I've often wondered—if we had rented a good modern cottage, would we ever have had Still Cove? In any case, she was wise, as she invariably was, for after the children married and had their own children, we spent more and more time on the Cape while they took turns at Stillmeadow during vacation times. Connie and Curt even rented a bus and brought a whole load of city children to experience the delight of country living, and some of them had never walked barefoot on sweet dewy grass in their whole lives!

I have described Cape living in my book *My Own Cape Cod.* Still Cove seems like an extension of Still-meadow, and the main problem is that I carry too much back and forth, including the heaviest old typewriter ever made and all Amber's traveling gear—kitty-litter pan, jars of food, favorite toys, brushes and combs, and vitamins. Erwin loads everything neatly at Stillmeadow, and David is waiting at the other end to unload. My dear neighbor Millie has the Cape refrigerator stocked. When I come back to Stillmeadow, Connie and Curt and Alice and Anne have the beloved old house shining, and the refrigerator jammed with delicacies.

On a clear day toward the end of winter, the sky is forever. It loses the flat look of bitter-cold days and seems to have a special promise. Even the birds fly differently, in widening circles instead of huddling. The air smells of melt instead of ice, and the buds on the lilacs are freshly varnished.

On such a day I drove to Cape Cod with Helen, Vicky, and Olive. The Cape house was glowing with sun, and Amber checked it with all the intensity of the FBI searching for imaginary criminals. Then she stretched out full length on the picture-window sill to toast herself. In the brilliance of the Cape light, her apricot fur seemed to give forth light.

The girls dashed to the beach like homing ducks. The ocean is perhaps the greatest magnet on this planet. Mountain people would argue about this, but I believe man's kinship with the sea is basic. The wideness of the great plains is another special mystery, but I feel I belong to the sea, and possibly it is because our forefathers crossed it to seek a new world.

My current Cape teen-ager came over to do a few chores, and once more I felt reassured about today's youth. Dave will never make headlines because he has bombed a bank or shot a policeman. He will not be picked up for drugs or stealing a car. He is what they call a square, and it is a pity that such boys do not make news, for there are plenty of them.

Dave is a big, solid boy, built like a football linebacker. He would make two of my dear Erwin. He has a very dark, fairly short mop of hair and deep eyes under a wide brow. He looks indeed as if there might be a touch of Indian somewhere in his background. Dave has a goal and knows where he is going. He wants to be a forester. He is a student at Cape Cod Community College and has no idea of complaining about it.

When he was eight, he told me, he loved fishing better than anything, but he has no time to fish any more, because he works when he isn't in school. The only thing he won't do is weed, because you never seem to get anywhere with that.

I had one difficulty when I first knew him, because I would have a list of chores that should last a whole afternoon, and I would hardly turn around before he loomed in the doorway grinning. "That's done," he would say. "What do I do now?"

When he raked the lawn, it sounded like Niagara Falls as the rake sped along, and when he cleaned out the fireplace, the quiet ashes really got a shock! Last summer, he and his father mowed ninety-one lawns,

and next summer Dave plans to do at least twenty-one
a week himself.

One Sunday he brought his girl friend to meet me,
a slim, quiet girl with hair only to her shoulders, and
both eyes plainly visible. She wore neat slacks and a
blouse with sleeves. And *shoes*. She sat in pleasant silence looking with adoration at Dave while he chatted
away on every subject known to man. When they left,
she said she had enjoyed seeing me.

That night there was one of those screaming teen-
age riots on television. Shaggy, barefoot boys and girls
were demonstrating against something, although it was
not clear whether it was Vietnam or the Establishment
or whatever college they were supposed to be attending.
I could not help feeling an ache of compassion for them
all, along with the usual question of why and where and
how this phenomenon came to darken our era.

Perhaps we adults are guilty of various things we
do not even understand, but we are certainly guilty of
headlining juvenile misdeeds. The teen-agers I love so
much will wait to get their pictures in the newspapers
for some achievement some years hence. They may
speak on television panels about politics or ecology or
what to do about the town dump. Meanwhile, they
quietly pursue undramatic courses.

I do not believe that any of us at any age can be
completely unbiased or entirely rational. We are woven
of countless threads, most of which we do not even know
about. Our heritage is peculiarly our own, and the
mystery of personality has never been catalogued by
any expert. Those of us who grew up in a quieter time
had some advantages, despite wars to end wars and a
major depression, because the basic pattern of develop-

ment was much the same for most people. How do we know what we would be like if we were nineteen and subject to the turmoil of today?

Perhaps the one universal solace for anyone, anytime, anywhere is being able to blame something or somebody for the sorry state of the world we find around us. Today's young people want to blame the older generation or the government, and the older folk find some ease in blaming the young. There must always be a scapegoat, and this evidently goes back to Biblical times. I notice men will do anything except ever, ever blame themselves.

My father had a simple theory. Anything that was wrong was the fault of the Democrats. He even, I suspect, had a sneaking suspicion that they affected the weather adversely. This was irrational, but at least he had one focus for his blame. Some of the young people today seem confused about whether they should bomb a bank or blow up Washington. Papa knew that, to keep things right, he could just vote Republican.

One young radical stated grandly that his group would abolish all work, all money, all the Establishment. Everyone would be free and happy. But first everything must be destroyed. Subsequently he had to accept the current state of law, for he was jailed for inciting to riot.

It seems to me a pity he did not have to work and live by his labor for a time, instead of on handouts from the affluent society he hates. Certainly I do not think jail ever stabilizes a personality.

The first sign of spring is the tips of the skunk cabbage at the lower edge of the pond, and what a miracle they are! They are almost a tropical green, and the tips look like cornucopias poking up through the lacy ice. The children watch for them and come leaping to the house in triumph when they see them. They have grown there since we first came to Connecticut, year in and year out, marking nature's calendar. I always wish they had a prettier name, although I am very fond of skunks.

The next thing I see is the dark stain of sap running down the trunk of the giant maples. The sap begins to rise on mild days and stops when the temperature plummets. Along the old road to Woodbury, men are getting out the sap spiles and buckets, and this is a happy sight.

In the country, I think, we live ahead of the seasons, for by now the houses are full of seed catalogues and windows are full of seedlings, although we have not said farewell to winter by any means. We simply feel the coming of another growing season, as the maples sense it is time to get ready for green leaves softening the dark line of branches. The trees have their own calendar, and no man can really explain it, for some winters last into April and some end in mid-March. True countrymen read the messages of nature not by weather reports, but in the land itself, and I have never known them to be wrong.

The Full Snow Moon is one of the loveliest; perhaps the crystalline air itself affects her. My friends Helen, Vicky, and Olive grow restless after supper and decide to walk in the moonlit woods, even if the temperature is zero. The shadows on the snow are like etchings, and the only sound is the occasional cracking of an icy branch. On such a night in the woods, they

feel a strange link with the universe and a renewal of
their own identity. When they come in, they bring the
smell of snow and pine and damp wool, and it takes a
little time before they are ready to get out the popcorn
and melt the butter and poke the fire.

In this age of tenseness, we all need such times to
renew our souls.

One feeling we all have in the valley is that, when
February comes, spring is just over the hill. "Well, it's a
short month," we say. "Won't be long now."

Actually February is twenty-eight days, except for an
extra one in leap year, and that isn't much shorter than
the months with thirty days. It adds up to forty-eight
hours less. But as far as we are concerned, February
isn't really long because of those two days. Which makes
me realize what a mystery "time" is.

We live by it generally; it marks our comings and
goings. It regulates the pattern of our days. But what is
time, really? We move back an hour in fall and ahead
an hour in spring, but where do those hours go? They
are not like stones dropped in a bottomless well. They
are, presumably, sixty minutes more or less according
to our clocks.

But nature has her own time, which is even more
mysterious. Sometimes grass is greening early, sometimes
late. April may be the end of winter or a beginning of
spring. Forces man cannot understand operate the
rhythm of the seasons. And in the country, we follow
nature's time even in planting the early peas. We set a
date for a party and may have to postpone it a week

because of a storm. Oscar Lovdal begins haying when nature's calendar says the hay is ripe for cutting.

In another area, our own clocks are useless. We all live through days that are as endless as if the earth had stopped turning. I have had a number of days during which grief erased all sense of the passing of the hours. Then there are days that are short as a love lyric—the sun seems to be setting before last night's moonlight has dimmed. Sorrow stops the clocks, and happiness sends them spinning like meteors.

But in our society we all watch the clock nevertheless. There are clocks in almost every room in the house, and practically everyone wears a wrist watch. Radio and television announce the time hour after hour, to be sure we know exactly what it is.

I sometimes wish we had only sundials, for most sundials are inscribed, "I only mark the hours that shine."

We have two antique clocks at Stillmeadow, one a steeple clock and one a shelf clock that has come down in the family for generations. A third is stored in my closet, because there is no extra mantel for it to rest on. My friend Pret Barker, who collects old clocks and is a researcher, tells me it was one of the very early ones made in Connecticut. I remember it at my grandfather's in West Springfield, Massachusetts, where it was repaired in 1906. It winds with a big key and operates by weights and actually has an alarm. It strikes the hours with a mellow tone.

Pret himself has a large collection of priceless clocks, all different, all in working order, scattered throughout the house. Each has its own music when it strikes, and since they do not all strike at the same second, it seems as if they are talking to one another. A good many lifetimes have been measured by these clocks, and I wish I knew about them all.

The modern electric clocks are not as romantic but are independent as long as the current is on. During a nor'easter or an ice storm, they suddenly stop, the hands motionless as if frozen. It gives me a strange feeling to go through the house and see time standing still, and habit is so strong that I look at every one in every room. If someone has remembered to wind the ancient ones, they keep ticking, but usually I have let them run down— even the one that goes thirty hours.

It reminds me, as many things do, that with all our expanding technocracy, we are not as independent as the early settlers. We even lack water when the pump stops working. The stove and the refrigerator and the furnace go off; the lights won't turn on. Push-button living is easy when all goes well. When power fails, as it sometimes does even in summer, we do not know how to manage.

At the farm we light the fire on the great hearth and bring out the oil lamps and find the candles, and I may say the house is never lovelier than when lighted by firelight and candlelight. We can cook over the hearth fire and use the chafing dish, and we can use canned heat for the old coffeepot. But during the longest blackout this winter, I sat up tending the fire until two in the morning. The next day I talked with a friend in the next town, which was not affected. Her remark was classic.

"I don't see why you sat up all night," she said.

"Why didn't you just turn on your electric blanket and get into bed?"

Toward the end of February the wood pile is at ebb tide. We begin gathering fallen branches along the road to the mailbox to help kindle the logs. There is, I note, a dreadful waste of good usable fuel all over the valley. People do not bother to pick it up. They buy synthetic logs instead. I always remember, when I drive down Jeremy Swamp Road and see the rotting logs and branches, how impressed I was when walking in the woods in Germany many years ago, because there was not one twig to pick up. The woods were as tidy as a Victorian parlor.

My friend Hal Borland might not approve of this, since he is a firm believer in leaving nature alone, and decaying wood goes back to nourish the earth. But I cannot help wishing the debris of winter could be carried in to make a fire warm an empty hearth.

About this time of year, more cats turn up at the back door, and my cat cafeteria is busier than ever. The regular customers I know very well. They belong to nobody but themselves, and they live in the few old barns left in this area. My three closest friends among them are respectively charcoal gray, gray and salt-and-pepper with white paws, and rusty orange. They do not want to come into the house, which is a good thing, since Amber would begin a modern battle of Waterloo. They do like me to stand at a decent distance and *talk* to them. Then they eat everything in sight and look at me gravely with wide-lidded eyes, twitching their ears to acknowledge that they know me.

When a new one joins the union, I do research to be sure he or she is not just a lost pet. At least two of them have perfectly good homes down the road a way and simply like the Stillmeadow menu. Cats, at least those I know, have a routine. So I am able to put out the leftover beef stew around the time when my neediest boarders are due. The house cats from up the line get the leftovers from the pan.

Amber loves to sit in the window and watch them and switch her tail madly, but she does not want them for playmates. Since she never watches herself in the mirror, I wonder how she knows these are her kinfolk? She feels a dog is really an odd mistake of nature, and takes a long time to accept even a docile one.

But when we raised cockers and cats and Irish setters all together, they felt they were all alike. The Siamese slept between the paws of the golden cocker. Puppies and cats cleaned up the Pablum bowls together. They arranged the territorial imperative among themselves, so that the Irish slept at the head of my bed, the cockers at the foot, with the cats tucked in between.

The fact is, nobody ever told our animals they couldn't live happily together. They had their individual differences. Holly liked her food soupy, but Teddy liked to crunch his. Esmé, the Siamese, liked imported sardines, but Tigger, the Manx, preferred plain chopped beef. Some of them loved eggs; some didn't. But as for communal life, they had no reservations. They liked it.

In many city schools nowadays, children from differing ethnic groups are gathered, and I find this a hopeful trend in modern education. It does mean extra work for teachers, especially when English is the second

language and home environments differ so widely, but I
believe the time to establish the fact of one nation, in-
divisible, is in the early school years.

Amber is shy of dogs for the simple reason that she
has not lived with one. Her few dog friends happen to
drop in with their owners often enough for her to get
used to them. She is also shy of people unless she sees
them a great deal, but she is quick to recognize the
sound of a special friend's car motor.

Back to my country cats. I notice they have pro-
tocol. One side of a bowl is for one cat, the other for
the next one. There is seldom a skirmish. After they eat,
they will line up on the warm step by the well house
and take good baths, scouring away at their bullet faces
with big, efficient paws. At dusk they vanish, each to his
own hideaway.

But when we get up in the morning, the first thing
we see through the kitchen window is a row of emerald,
onyx, amber eyes as the boarders line up for breakfast.

When I dish up their meals, I find my thoughts
going to an anonymous letter from a reader of my book
about Amber. Hate mail is a curious phenomenon, and
since I am not what could be called a controversial
writer, I do not get much of it. This one was two pages
of vicious attack on me for writing about a pedigreed
cat instead of championing the cause of stray cats. Actually my first cats were a paper bag full of kittens I found
on the way home from school one day when I was very
young, and wherever I have lived, cats have had a way
of turning up on my doorstep.

But of course I could not explain this to the letter
writer, since even the postmark was smudged. I commented on it to the line of cat boarders at the back

door, but the beef stew was more interesting to them. Then I sat by the kitchen window with my pedigreed Abyssinian and discussed with her the fact that her descent from the royal cats of Egypt made her an object of hatred. She was too busy scrubbing her ears, turning them inside out, and polishing to answer.

My feeling about hate mail is that it has nothing to do with reality. It is a projection of some inner state of the writer and may indicate tensions and emotional turmoil. I cannot imagine being upset by it, although I have a couple of author friends who worry for weeks about a hostile letter.

I notice much of the reader mail in the magazines and newspapers divides neatly into two parts. A few careful correspondents point out why an opposite point of view as to weapon increases, national programs, student unrest, or whatever, is feasible. But more adverse mail seems to be written by people who have not really read what they are blasting about. And a sad aspect of mankind, at least in our country, is that we are not always ready to discuss issues. We cannot hear when we shout.

I admit I was tempted to lose what they call my cool when a reviewer of the Cape Cod book, on which I had worked about five years, found a fatal flaw. I suggested paprika on clam chowder. I still think chowder looks pretty with a dash of paprika.

And as my stray cats turn up, they continue to find the welcome mat out, well furnished with warm dinners.

One aspect of life that interests me most is that it is never the same day after day. A friend once said, "Life is so daily," and although I cherish that statement, I find every day has something new to observe or feel. Even when I am snowbound I look out the window, and the birds play out a drama against the falling snow that is never quite like the one during the last storm. And there are always new footprints on the snow, some familiar, like those of the skunks, who leave a special track where the tail drags, and some others that are impossible to identify.

Shadows on the snow are never exactly the same as yesterday's. And no two fires in the great fireplace are duplicates. Perhaps the only constant thing in life is change.

I thought about this as I was engaged in an activity I never would have dreamed of a few years ago. I was mending a necklace for my Cape Cod friend David while he washed the kitchen ceiling. David had been visiting in the South Sea Islands and came home with a long chocolate-colored necklace of some kind of seeds. It broke while he was shoveling snow.

"I feel bad about it," he said.

I managed to sew it together, really praying for success, for I am no expert at any needlework, much less threading seeds.

"I am going to wear it under my jersey," he said, "and be careful."

And then he was off for a hockey game.

Obviously, this particular string of seeds held the memories of his visit in the Islands. And I suddenly thought what Papa would say about a young man wearing a necklace. We have come a long way in a relatively short time!

Dave has taught me a great deal about today's

young. On the surface he looks like one of the gang. His shining dark eyes peer at me through a fall of shining dark hair bound with one of those Indian headband affairs which does keep the sweat from his eyes in summer. His big masculine frame is clad in worn jeans. (If he bought a new pair, he would have to smear it with paint or oil.) His jersey hangs loose, but he has a belt with a fancy medallion on it. And his shoes—well, it is best not to describe them.

But underneath resides a gentle, thoughtful, serious boy sparked with a keen sense of humor. His manners and language are definitely square, although he might hate me for saying so. Also, it is impossible for him to lounge around in the current fashion. When there is nothing special to do, he will think of something and leap off to feed the birds an extra meal or clean the inside of the car or wash out the skunks' water dish and put out their food. Or decide he might run down and check on the mail or get some fresh cream for Amber at the store.

"I may as well do it while I have time," he says.

His natural interest in learning about anything new is a constant delight to me, since I am certainly a frustrated teacher. Together we identify birds with as much excitement as if we were seeing UFO's. I read Peterson's book while he races around with the binoculars and his camera swinging around his neck.

He is more interested in how I write books than most of my friends are. And since he got over being afraid to get out of his car when Blackberry was in the yard, he has become one of my skunk's best friends. As for Amber, he is very careful not to make sudden noises to scare her and often turns up with an extra package of thinly sliced roast beef for her which only one market carries.

He is now wondering about cooking.

"How do you cook a steak?" he asked. "Can I just fry it? And how long?"

He tossed back his hair so he could look at me while I explained about steak.

Much as I dislike long hair on boys or men, it is probably a part of some inner urge to which they respond. With some of the young men I know, it is impossible to tell what they look like behind the wall of fur, but if it gives them a sense of being with-it, as they say, we should reconcile ourselves and hope the fashion will change before long.

The very young are a constant surprise. Anne, my granddaughter, is eleven. Last weekend her mother reported that Anne was visiting one of her best friends on a Long Island estate. It was complete with Olympic swimming pool, vast greenhouses, stable, tennis courts, and an entrance, said Anne, like Hampton Court. (Anne is quite fond of the Elizabethan era.) They swam at night, had fresh-picked strawberries, slept in four-posters like royal beds, and were served elegant drinks of ginger ale and lemon by the French butler. He also built fires in the library for them when they made doll clothes in the morning.

"Imagine," said Anne. "Fires lighted in the morning!"

When she came home late Sunday night, she

crawled happily into her little bed in the corner of her room.

"Well," she said, "so much for glamour! It's nice to be home."

I am sure Anne, whatever happens to her in her life, will face it with equanimity—and never be over-powered. I can imagine her being entertained at the White House and telling the President that what she would really like to do is visit the kennels and see the dogs.

Alice, at thirteen (going on fourteen, she says firmly), has experienced the excitement of being in the "Nutcracker" ballet in New York City as well as play-ing the violin in an orchestra, which she takes as a matter of course.

When I grew up in a small town in Wisconsin, we never even saw a ballet. High-school plays were the only occasions when we appeared in public. Children have more opportunities these days. Recently, for instance, I heard a young teenager on television who is a profes-sional weatherman in Oregon. He explained about isobars and so on. Another thirteen-year-old was a guest performer at the Boston Symphony and received a standing ovation. He played solo violin for most of the concert.

Children have certainly been liberated.

There is nothing more difficult than writing about the children in the family. An objective view is impos-sible, and the temptation to be sentimental is over-whelming. Besides there is the matter of time. My life with the children can never be pinpointed at one stage of their lives or mine. This, of course, is what the

Women's Lib women would never understand. Every day, every hour, a child grows and changes, and most of us unliberated women do not want to miss one bit of it.

When Connie and Barbara and David went away to college—different colleges—they came home for vacations like guests, for they had been living in an exciting and different world. This is the period, I suspect, most difficult for parents. Suddenly the sons and daughters are separate individuals. Jill and I felt lost and also timid.

Someone recently told me I was a very private person, and I realized that this description really fitted Connie more than me. She was never one to pour out confidences. She was slim and fair with eyes the color of the sea on a quiet day. Her voice was musical and had a faint overtone from the years we lived in Virginia that was soft and pleasing.

Barbara moved in a constant drama. She was thin but bouncing with vitality. With her dark hair and wide, shining, deep-blue eyes and lovely mobile mouth, she provided excitement from the early days when every angleworm was a snake. From her Aunt Heloise she inherited an addiction to causes—almost any cause that would help someone. We called her our crusader.

David was always so thin we felt we could see through him. He had his father's penetrating gaze and his father's inimitable sense of humor. His dark hair grew in all directions. His voice had the easy, level tones of his mother's, and, like Jill, he was always able to see both sides of every question. For the girls there was only one side, and that was theirs. David seldom talked except when he was a small boy and had frightening asthma attacks at midnight.

I used to get up, heat the steam kettle, and drape a big bath towel over his head while we sat at the kitchen counter. It was always between one and two in the morning before the attack lessened. The room was steamy and hot, but I could look out of the window at the cool moonlit night. David talked whenever he could get his breath, because he felt he should entertain me. When he began to recover, he wiped his pale, wet face and stood up. He always said, "Thank you. I am sorry I had to wake you up."

We finally sent him to a camp at the seashore during the worst of the haying season, although he did not want to leave the farm. He not only felt shy but was desperately afraid of water. He would not even dip into the pond with the girls. As we grew nearer to camp, he sat folded up tightly. We tried to converse, but there was no response. Finally we drew up before a roadside stand offering him the comfort of ice cream.

"I don't want any," he mumbled.

We did not look back when we left him. Jill had what I called her stony Scotch look, and I was crying. The first time we were allowed to visit him, we had decided he must come home. The gentle, warm Macs who ran the camp met us.

"Where's David?" I asked, feeling sure he was lying on a cot lifeless.

"Oh, he's out swimming," said Mr. Mac. "I'll get him in."

Another one of those best memories was stored as David came running out of the water waving his arms and shouting. "Hey, Mom, I can swim! Mr. Mac says I am just one of those people who cannot sink!"

He condescended to visit briefly, then plunged back into the sea.

I can see him now, over six feet tall, broad-shouldered and rugged, I still also see the thin, leggy boy splashing in the surf. He married a gentle, quiet girl who successfully concealed from us the fact that she could write an article so difficult none of us could understand it. We were in awe of her. When their three children came along, we felt easier because we had much in common then. But she still looks like one of those ethereal gentlewomen in one of those early oil paintings.

When Connie and Barbara first went away to college, we did our best to cope with the emptiness, as all parents must. Jill kept on planting more vegetables than we could ever use, making a quiet garden for me, training the cockers and Irish for obedience shows. I spent most of the time at the typewriter or cooking special dishes or trying to get the oxblood red paint off an old sea chest. David went off to Cornell but fortunately was near enough to drop in for weekends with his various friends.

The old house was full of company most of the time, but as much as we loved our dear friends and neighbors, we kept marking the calendars with homecoming dates for the three and, when they came, trying to act casual about arrivals and departures.

One friend commented over dinner one night, "I know it is nice to have some peace and quiet." We never seemed to relish peace and quiet.

The time came when the girls brought what they called dates home on holidays. They were all kinds, and at the start Jill made one of her pronouncements about them.

"We must never criticize a single one," she said, "or we are lost."

Only at midnight, after one weekend, she said fiercely, "If Barbara doesn't marry Val, we are going to adopt him. That's flat!"

And later on, I told Val—but not until they were married. He grinned and said, "I knew you would."

I was especially careful while Curt was courting Connie, but when they were married, Curt acquired along with his bride a mother-in-law who did not fit the usual mother-in-law jokes. In fact, Connie complained I always took his side in any argument. Our own disagreements are limited to deciding whether it is better to try a field goal on the last down or a pass.

The seven grandchildren deserve a book by themselves. As I write, the main problem is whether this is the time for my eleven-year-old Anne to have her first cocker puppy and whether David's thirteen-year-old son will always have a pet cobra.

I wonder just when the ground-hog legend began. It is certainly old, and although I am told the ground hog has no idea whether it will be spring or not, most legends have some basis in fact. So some farmer once saw a ground hog in February, and there were six weeks of winter afterward, and spring was early, and he remembered the ground hog, and the legend was born. It belongs in the same category as the woolly caterpillars who foretell winter by the width of the black band in their middles.

But the first announcement that spring is coming

is the pussy willow. The soft, dove-gray buds (or catkins) herald the end of winter along with the skunk cabbage. Also we watch for the lilac buds to swell and look varnished and for a pale glow in the willows by the pond. And, to me, the air feels lighter even if snow is falling. Everything in nature seems to be softening— even the maples, which now have a pinky look in the branches. Color begins to appear in the swamp so the country looks more like a pastel than an etching.

The major effect on me is to want the storm windows off, which is certainly ridiculous, for the long cold will not be over until mid-March, and there will be sleet and snow and sharp winds roaring. March is home to all the winds. They are important, too, for they help diminish the snowdrifts and break up the pond ice. In nature, everything is related in a way that is awesome to contemplate.

The snow has protected the earth all winter. Experts now believe it contains life-giving qualities, but I cannot name them. Now countless small shoots are ready to push up, and the wind helps as it roars down from eternity (or seems to). After the snow is gone, the wind dries out the sea of mud that blankets the valley.

And so we move along toward spring, until she becomes a dream realized.

February in New England is our most variable month. It must be lived day by day to be understood— and then who really does understand it? Today, for instance, I went down to the pond to see the first sign of spring, the skunk cabbage. The pond was a skim of ice, and the two golden willows at the end looked like a charcoal sketch. I stopped to speak to them, for they

are my favorites. Leafless, their branches seem to flow
to the pond edge in a rhythm like music. Jill planted
them when we first came to Stillmeadow, and they were
two spindly little spikes. Now when they bloom, the
sky turns to gold.

I stood thinking about those early days when we
worked day and night trying to fix up the old farmhouse
where nobody but rats had lived for a long time. All the
plumbing was cracked. The wide black-oak floors had
holes in every room, and some former tenant had tacked
cigarette tins over the biggest gaps. The kitchen had
an iron range, very rusty, and a lead-lined sink. But the
great fireplace in the keeping room was big enough for
Jill's son to stand up in. Some windows were broken;
one door shut only if you hammered it. The yard was
a tangle of weeds, and we mowed with a scythe.

But we loved it, and so did the three children, the
Irish setter, the cockers, and the cats. And we built
memories in it in a way one cannot do in a spanking
new house. I believe what you get from a home is what
you put in of yourself, and today I decided the willows
mean more to me because we planted them than even
the giant sugar maples that surround the house itself,
much as we cherish them. They were planted by some
very early owner, if not the man who built Stillmeadow,
and at night they catch the stars in their top branches.
Now in February the great trunks have black rivers of
sap flowing gently to the ground.

One year at the end of February, we hung buckets
on spiles in those trunks and learned to appreciate maple
syrup. After days and nights of lugging sap and boiling
it down, we had four pints of pale gold syrup, and no

wallpaper left on the walls of the front parlor. From then on we bought our syrup, and I still do, at the Stiles farm down the Woodbury Road.

Now my thoughts turn back to the skunk cabbage and the several shiny emerald points thrusting through the snow. The skunk cabbage is a miracle, for it opens in a kind of cornucopia shape and looks like a tropical plant, and in a winter world it is really the flag of spring. Ours has always been at the lower edge of the pond and nowhere else. I bent over and greeted it, and I am glad to say I am no longer considered mad because I talk to growing things. Jill once asked me not to tell strangers who came to call that the reason my African violets were spectacular was the long conversations I held with them.

For now the scientists have decided plants have feelings, too, and in tests have found that plants talked to doubled in size, while those ignored simply died. One expert of late thinks vegetables also have feelings, but this rather worries me, for I hate to think of apologizing to a carrot for cooking it. I have trouble enough with fish or lobsters, and if guests will not cook them, I put the lobsters into a brown paper sack and drop the whole thing in, trying to remember that lobsters once caught are going to be eaten by someone.

When I came back to the house, the yard was deep with birds, and even the shy pair of cardinals stayed by the feeder. They actually blaze against the white snow. They are shy birds, but the bonny little black-capped chickadees will almost eat out of the youngest grandchild's hand. They are my favorites, because they keep on chirping away all day long. The nuthatches make me dizzy, for they run head-down on the tree trunks and eat upside down too.

Connie says I spend more time on the wildlife than on the family, in which she includes waiting on the stray barn cats—and the three skunks and two raccoons who want to be served at night. We seldom see the deer any more, for our valley is suffering from the onrush of civilization, but Curt did see a big buck when he was way up in our wood gathering dead branches for the fireplace. The grandchildren, Alice and Anne, trudge through the woods in the deep snow to find wild-animal tracks and are especially happy when they see the bobcat paw marks. In the pond we have muskrats and occasionally an otter, although otters were all but exterminated some years ago when the pelts were worth five dollars. Beavers went the same sad way but are coming back.

As I approached the house, I found my favorite barn cat by the well, washing her big blocky face, so I heated more milk and dished up some beef stew. If I did not, she would jump to the outside window box and stare at me with shining green eyes. Then Amber would fling herself against the window inside and utter sounds bigger than her whole five pounds. She cannot stand another cat. She reminds me of some women who must always be at center stage.

By the time the outside cat was fed, snow was falling, and it was winter once more. The back kitchen smelled of rubbers and mittens and jackets, and Curt was building up the fire. We burn our own wood from the upper woodlot, chiefly fallen branches. Nature does not waste anything, and I wish mankind could learn this vital lesson once and for all. Unfortunately, mankind seems bent on destruction most of the time.

We have two cherished neighbors, the Lovdals,

who still farm, and I find it reassuring to go into Oscar's barn and see the beautiful black-and-white cows smelling of spicy hay and warm, rich milk. When we first came to the valley, it was settled by working farmers. Now many of the children's guests who come out from the city have never seen a cow.

The Lovdals dropped in for a hot toddy as the snow thickened, and I had made our favorite Sausage-Cheese Balls. This recipe is not in my new cookbook, as it was sent to me by Vicki Robertson too late for me to tuck it in. I shall never, never write another cookbook, but I shall share this every time I can.

To make the cheese balls, use 1 package of coon cheese (Kraft's), 1 pound of hot sausage, and 3 cups of biscuit mix (Bisquick). Melt the cheese in the double boiler, add the sausage, and mix well. Pour into a large mixing bowl, add the Bisquick, and mix well (you may use your hands). Make into small balls (¾ inch) and bake on a cooky sheet at 350 degrees for 15 minutes or until lightly browned. They may be mixed ahead and frozen before cooking. Freeze on cooky sheets, then pop into a plastic bag and return to the freezer. Thaw before baking.

Valentine's Day is important in our family. The grandchildren make the valentines, and we use pink candles on the trestle table and add a bouquet of pink roses from the village flower shop. Curt does the steak in the fireplace, and we have cake with pink icing for dessert. I like sentimental valentines and am sorry to see so many funny ones in general use. It is nice to be sentimental once in a while.

The Full Snow Moon rises on the seventeenth over

the swamp, and surely nothing is lovelier than moon-light on new-fallen snow. The children want to go out in the night and feel the mystery. I am satisfied to stand in the door and say good night to the world. February is a short month, often bitter and wild, but it also has the Thaw, which is the promise of spring to come.

SPRING

Mw.arch came in snorting like a lion. As I
looked out of the window, I saw the pond still glimmer-
ing with ice except where the ink-black water flowed
over the rocky dam. I sat down with my coffee and
watched the water trying to free itself. The pond, I told
Amber, believes in spring. Winter is long and hard in
my New England valley, and I myself want to be free of
it. The brook that plunges down through the woods and
the old apple orchard vanishes under the ice at the upper
end of the pond, and George's brook across the road
makes music in her stony bed.

When I go out to feed the barn cats, I see Jeremy
Swamp standing knee-deep in water but fringed with ice
lace. The ancient stone fence along the winding road
has a polished look, and the road itself, of course, runs
with water. Perhaps water is the true symbol of March,
along with mud. The yard around Stillmeadow alternately thaws and freezes, and when we walk to the picket
fence to greet weekend guests, we sink ankle deep.

Sunlight is thin and the sky more often billows
with clouds—dark, heavy clouds burdened with more

rain. The way they move is always mysterious to me, as if they had a destination they must reach at some certain moment. When there is a break in them, the world is dipped in pale gold.

At the village market everyone is gay because, as George Tomey says, it is *not snowing!* And Jean Lovdal says a flock of robins is back at Drumlin Farm. My news is that the lilac buds are swelling, and I picked a bunch of snowdrops in the garden. Snowdrops are delicate, but their fragile white bells pay no attention to the March winds. Every bell has faint green striations, as if nature wanted a final touch of elegance. When I gather the first handful, I put it in a very old milk-glass salt shaker to brighten the keeping room. And I like to remember the first spring we were at Stillmeadow, and Jill called the three children to come quickly—we had snowdrops by the well house, a present from the past.

I notice we valley dwellers sense the coming of spring, and most of us begin cleaning out closets and sorting out the accumulations of winter. Out go those unmatched mittens, single snow boots, ragged woolen socks. Alice and Anne want to put the sleds and skates away and get out the small boat for the pond—much too early. My son-in-law vanishes into the woods and comes back lugging fallen branches much too wet to burn.

I am more and more eager to get the storm windows off, although the house will need them another month. I purely hate storm windows, for I do not want an extra thickness of glass between me and my world outside. The storm windows are nailed on most of the 12″ by 8″ small-paned windows about the middle of October. No two windows are the same size, and we originally nailed number tags on each one, but by now we never can find the right markers anyway, so the storm sash gets un-nailed (if there is such a word) and stacked at random in the storage house. Next fall we shall struggle to match them up, but right now who cares about next fall?

Connie thinks we should do over the kitchen cup-boards. "Pretty soon, Mama," she says, "we'll have the house full every single weekend. Better stock up the shelves." I sort the herbs and discard the old ones. Herbs tend to lose both color and savor after a time, which some people don't realize. Parsley gets pale and lifeless, paprika cakes in the container, bay leaves turn brown-ish, and so on. Nothing renews my interest in cooking like a whole shelf of fresh herbs. Experts advise a cool, dark place for them, but my nearest such place is the cellarway halfway across the house. Since that is reserved for emergency supplies, my herbs stay right by the stove.

Our favorite supper on a windy March night is Jean's Country-Baked Spareribs. It calls for 4 to 6 pounds of spareribs, cracked through the center, then cut in serving pieces and broiled until brown on both sides. With the fat drained off, pour over the following mixture: 2 bouillon cubes dissolved in 2 cups boiling water, ¼ cup hot catsup, 3 tablespoons Worcestershire sauce, 1 tablespoon vinegar, ½ teaspoon cayenne pepper, ½ teaspoon celery salt, 3 whole cloves, 3 whole allspice, ½ bay leaf, 1 medium onion, sliced. Cover the ribs and sauce with foil and bake until fork-tender, about 2 hours. This serves four to six.

This is my kind of recipe, for it can be made ahead of time, and after it is tucked in the oven can be left to itself except for an occasional peek. It's good with baked potatoes or noodles or dumplings or crusty French bread for dunking. A tossed salad is best and fruit for dessert and/or cheese and crackers.

Another favorite is Barbara Lovely's Minestrone, which is made as follows: 1 pound summer squash, sliced thin; 1 pound zucchini, sliced thin; 1 package frozen green beans, cut; 1 cup fresh or frozen green peas (never canned); 1 No. 2 size can tomatoes and juice, or equivalent in fresh tomatoes; 2 cups fresh green cabbage, cut in strips or squares (1 inch); 1/4 pound salt pork, minced; 3 large onions, diced; 1/4 teaspoon garlic salt, or to taste; 3 tablespoons olive oil; 1 cup thin spaghetti, broken into two-inch lengths; and salt and pepper.

Prepare all the vegetables and have at hand. Mince the salt pork finely and put into a heavy stew pot over low heat. As fat accumulates, add the diced onions and cook until soft and yellow, not brown. Add a quart or two of water, the squash, zucchini, and green beans. Cook the spaghetti separately until almost done. Drain and have at hand. Cook the peas separately in a very little water. Drain and have at hand. When the squash and beans are almost done, add the tomatoes and juice. Bring back to a boil, add the cabbage, and cook about 8 to 10 minutes more. Add the peas and spaghetti. Add the olive oil and salt and pepper to taste. Serve with hot, crusty bread. Sprinkle with Parmesan cheese.

I myself hate dicing things or shredding them or chopping and beating, but when Alice says shyly, "Gram, this is the best I ever ate," I find any trouble well worth it. And actually nowadays there are so many aids when cooking—for instance, I remember Mama sifting flour three or four times, and who does that now? And she had to dry and bottle most of her own herbs while I can choose from dozens and dozens in the supermarket. All the bottled sauces are a special blessing. I do like making chili sauce and chutney and bread-and-butter pickles, but only when I have time and do it for fun. Usually I reach up to the cupboard and pull out whatever I need.

I have definite ideas about entertaining. I love soufflés but never have them when company comes unless there is room enough in the kitchen for the guests to gather while the soufflé cooks. Most of us, I think, have been dinner guests at homes where the hostess never has a chance to visit, as she is always in the kitchen working. It's more fun if the dinner is something she could do ahead of time so she can be a member of the party.

I deplore a dinner where the hostess leaps in and out during the whole meal. Genuine conversation is impossible. And, after all, it is the talk that should nourish the spirit, no matter what is on the platter. When I make out a menu for my favorite friends, I cross off anything that might mean I would be in the kitchen at the wrong time. I make an exception for steak, but we do that on the outdoor barbecue in season or my son-in-law does it over coals in the fireplace.

As March draws to a close, I admit few advertising enthusiasts would recommend it in New England for a vacation. As I write, sleet, mixed with snow and rain, beats against the window. But when I open the door and look out, I smell the clean, sweet air, and I hear the brook running down the hill, and I feel spring in my heart. March is a special gift from nature to restore and nourish the land, and without it roses would never bloom so beautifully in June. I shall be grateful to March when I bring in my first armful of dawn roses.

March brings a change in the rhythm of living in the valley. We feel spring is coming, although snow may be slanting down over the swamp, and the wind is dipped in ice. At the market I notice customers buy casually in the belief they can get out again tomorrow. On a day of melt, an eager neighbor has blankets airing on the line. Our spirits rise as the sap rises, and when I see the dark stain on my sugar maples, I happily start to make lists of spring chores.

I reflect, as I put out the food for the stray cats, that we follow nature's pattern in the country; we do not, ever, make our own. And perhaps the character of rural dwellers is built on this acceptance. In any case, most of us are less tense and driven than our city friends.

"Wait and see how the weather is," says Jean. "If it is bad, come tomorrow instead."

"I'll be over to fix the bathroom leak," says Art, "unless somebody's furnace goes off."

"I'll get in some more wood," Erwin remarks, "if it melts enough."

When I drive to Woodbury and see the shining sugar buckets on the maples, I feel the surge of spring in my very bones. At the Stiles farm, the early sap makes the pale, honey-colored syrup we all prize, and we buy pint or quart jars as we dream of buttermilk pancakes. The later run is dark and is what one buys commercially, and Mr. Stiles always apologizes for it when that time comes. The Stiles farm has been the prime source of maple syrup for longer than one can estimate, and I believe, if those frenetic highway people ever projected leveling the house and barns to make one more through-way, the whole valley would stage a revolution.

Southbury is no longer a quiet country village as it was, and those of us who watch the death of a rural area feel heartbreak. The deep woods crash, marshes are flooded, sweet-running trout streams polluted. Factories encroach. Chain stores plan to move in. A turnpike slices the wild-flower meadows.

Sometimes I think progress is man's greatest enemy. But I am thankful my own woods and swamps and streams are still safe, and nobody at the moment can drain my pond and build a development there. It belongs to the wildlife and the children. Our main worry is how to keep the muskrats from completely eroding the far bank and the beavers from building dams.

Deer are scarce, but the upper woods still make a refuge for them, and we do have one bobcat, although the grandchildren, Alice and Anne, have never seen him. They did find his lair in the rocky ledge beyond the swamp, but I was the fortunate one actually to watch him skimming along the edge of the swamp at dusk.

Raccoons come to the back door at night and eat whatever the cats have left. If you turn the light on suddenly, several pairs of shining emerald eyes stare at you. They are the most intelligent of the wild people, according to Sterling North, and we know it. They can use their paws like hands, and they figure out how to unlock any can lid, open any bird feeder, and would have no difficulty with the storm door if let alone.

The squirrels are hungry now; so are the winter birds. And before the ground is thawed, there are the robins, always too early for their own good. Food is scarce, because those juicy worms are under the frozen soil, but robins persist in believing in spring. They even sing on sunny days, and they manage somehow, for I have never seen starved ones in the yard.

A walk up the road to the mailbox when the March wind blows somehow reminds me of the days when spring tonics were doled out to families. Folks haven't changed much, except that now we dash to the drugstore for various vitamins that will take care of everything, or sprays for sinus aches or coughs or colds. Remedies were certainly more colorful in former days.

For a pain in ye head, says one of my favorites, you mix 2 ounces of rhubarb leaves sliced, 1 ounce Jesuit's bark in powder, 2 ounces of sugar candy, 2 drams of juniper berries, Sinnamon (sic) and nutmeg, a dram of each. Infuse this in a quart of strong wine.

For a cough or could (sic) take 4 ounces of candy syrup, 1 ounce of Spyrmisiti, and ¾ ounce of saltpeter.

For asthma—gunpowder and brimstone brused (sic) fine and mixt with treacle into a ball or stiff paste and take a little at pleasure.

Vigor is increased by a brew consisting of rice with sparrows' eggs boiled in milk together with honey and ghee.

Some of the remedies were worse than the ailment, I decide, especially those for convulsions, consumption, deafness, and so on, which called for snake oil, gander's fat, the blood and skin of a hare, crocodile oil. But a good many of them had enough rum or spirits or strong wine to make the sufferer feel no pain.

Man's search for cures has come a long way, to be

sure, yet whoever first decided leaves of digitalis were good for heart trouble was pretty wise after all. So we do learn from the past even if we have abandoned sulphur and molasses as a spring tonic. And I am thankful castor oil is no longer spooned out to hapless children as it was in my early childhood.

But one of my favorite friends is discouraged because the local drugstore does not carry Mothersill's seasick remedy.

On the way back from the mailbox, we can see water standing in the swamp with only a filament of ice in places, and the skunk cabbage is already thrusting taller cornucopias of green along the edge. The swamp bushes have color in their branches as the living sap rises. The great willows by the pond seem to give forth light, and finally the first peepers announce the end of winter, their tiny throats swelling with triumph.

I myself need the reassurance of spring after the long, cold winter. I feel my heart lighten. After all, I reflect as I put the soup kettle on, I am also a child of nature and must respond to her rhythm. I know a wet, heavy snow will melt before long. I know the lilac buds are already swelling, and some of the trees lose their starkness as faint color blurs the tips.

I battle the mud with better grace—and, oh, how muddy March can be! Mud can be ankle deep on the path to the pond and on the walk to the picket fence. Our soil at Stillmeadow is clay and what we call "loom," unlike the sandy soil of Cape Cod. It dries out slowly and is almost like cement when you try to scrape it from shoes or boots. We live with it; we can do nothing else. The old wide floor boards are impossible to keep shining. The car stands hub deep in it, and getting into that car requires the agility of a chamois as I leap from one soupy spot to another.

But it is heartening to think all that mud gradually lets moisture down to hungry frozen roots, enriches the land, and makes the greening earth possible. So who cares? It is all a part of nature's mysterious wisdom, a renewal and replenishing. And mankind has not yet been able to corrupt this plan.

The grandchildren are full of spring's excitement. They find tiny buds about to open in the border, so the snowdrops will bloom any minute, snow or not. They find where the wild violets will be growing green. They find polished stones that have worked their way up through the ice, and beautiful they are indeed, small presents from the great glacier of how many million years ago?

It is a happy time, and April is just up the hill!

The folder said, "Why Your Family?"

Well, it seems I was chosen as one of 17,000 out of 63 million to be investigated by the Census Bureau. It's strictly confidential, I was assured, for the census bureau is *airtight against snoopers.*

The lady agent, Mrs. S., carried in what can only be called a tome, whose contents were pages with lines and spaces to be filled in about me. I guessed there were at least thirty or forty pages.

As a writer, I have been interviewed for years by reporters, radio MCs, and various clubwomen, and I have never objected, feeling that I have no secret life. In fact, the only things under my rugs are occasional sour bugs which love to go under rugs. But suddenly I began to wonder, and I did not want to fill all those pages about my way of living. We live in a climate of fear nowadays, second only to Communist countries. Newsmen go to jail rather than divulge the source of their special information. Houses are wired, telephones tapped, and the FBI has files of millions of names, innocent or not. The Watergate incident came to my mind as Mrs. S. took out her pen.

So I began by finding out where she was born, where she now lives, how many families she interviews (40). I learned that it cost her thirty-five dollars to rent a tuxedo for her son's junior prom, that she has two dogs and two cats, all strays, that her mother was born in Litchfield but her aunt lives in Stonington.

Then we got to page one. Now the information wanted by the bureau is about clothing and linens, auto expenses and repairs, trips and vacations, utilities, fuels, household help, repairs to appliances, TVs, etc., home repairs and improvements, insurance, and a few other items.

An hour and a half later I needed an ice pack on my head. Unfortunately, I did not know how old my toaster was, when I had last bought sheets and pillowcases, how old my car was (this never came out right, since I bought the last one of a model the week before the new ones appeared). I had no records of when I bought my TV set (but it *was* black-and-white, which she wrote down). I remembered that my electric range was a little over a year old (just old enough so the warranty had run out when the timer blew).

Trips and vacations drew a blank, as I never take

them. I confessed that I have only one typewriter, non-electric. And no humidifiers. I forgot my one old electric fan. I had not bought any new clothes or rented any. And I did not know how much I had spent on food. No hospital expenses. I said I needed a new sofa because the springs were sagging in mine but I did not remember when I bought it or when it was re-covered.

By now I began to feel like someone who should be applying for welfare. I could not, afterward, remember all the things I did not have, but there were certainly a lot of them. And yet it seemed queer that I have four radios and a stereo—but no projector.

Books are evidently of no interest to the Census Bureau, and I must have several hundred at least, over-flowing the bookshelves and stacked in piles in closets. Never mind. I had *not* bought a new coat this year. Or new shoes.

As she got up to go, Mrs. S. handed me a blue tome just like the one she had been madly flipping the pages in and said cheerily, "I have to see you three times during the year. I'll be back in May, and meanwhile you can be filling this out."

I began to wonder how much 17,000 of these elegant portfolios, complete with pad and pencil and glassy pockets, must cost our rich government and how much this investigation cost and how far that money would go for food for the poverty areas. I was strongly tempted to write a letter to the director of the Census Bureau and ask for some information from him (including how much he spent during the year on house furnishings and vacations). But I had already lost half a day's work and had a headache, so I went to the kitchen (how old is my refrigerator?) and got out a good steak to thaw for supper (how much did I pay for that?).

I do know in this age we are not expected to have or want any privacy, but I wonder if it isn't time for a change before we all become statistics fed into a computer?

The more I think about this census, the more confused I find myself. Apparently names are chosen at random. Certainly I am not a typical American family. I am a countrywoman and a writer, but I do not farm, and I do not get interviewed on talk shows. I might be called a typical dog- and cat-lover and bird watcher and nature addict, but I was not asked how much it costs me per week for dog, cat, and bird food.

Now I am supposed to keep track of everything I spend in the next three months (minus the above categories), and I have never had any head for figures. How I admire my few friends who do budget, know what they spend and what they have left. I have no idea how much I spend on meat, for example; I buy what I need at the market. My tax man figures out my taxes, but I cannot imagine him following me around for three months with that huge blue record book. Even if I could cope with figures and knew to a penny what I did spend and *for what*, I would have no time or energy to write another book, which is a full-time job for me.

My best solution, I think, is not to buy anything in the next three months or have anything repaired or have the trim painted at Stillmeadow. But then the government's money would be spent in vain. Perhaps I should buy a humidifier, color TV set, new car, and so on, up to and including an electric toothbrush, not forgetting an electric rotisserie (we always cook in the fireplace).

I find this whole project more and more disturbing. At what point can a citizen of our great country have any privacy? Are we by any chance tending toward an era when the government will regulate our whole lives? I wonder if I were to say, "I do not wish to be in the census, thank you. Try my neighbors down the road"— would I make the FBI files?

I am too docile ever to know.

One controversy in the highly controversial era is that between those who love only cats and those who love only dogs. "I love dogs but I can't stand cats" is a statement I often hear. Or "I hate dogs, but I adore cats."

I stand firmly on my belief that both dogs and cats give richness to life, and both have been invaluable to mankind down the ages. Historians agree that dogs moved into man's orbit in primitive days when they helped hunt, warned of the approach of enemies, and fought off marauding wildlife. In return, bones and scraps were tossed to them, and they shared the warmth of the first fires. Gradually they became part of the family clan.

As for cats, it was cats who saved Egypt from starvation during a period when rats demolished the grain supplies. Cats were imported from Abyssinia and became so valuable that they moved into the palaces. At one. time a man who injured a cat had his eyebrows shaved off. When the cats died, they were embalmed and were put in the tombs of the Pharaohs along with jewels, garments, and stores of food to help masters in their journey to the land of the gods. There was even a cat goddess, and a good many bas-reliefs picture her.

So as far as service to mankind goes, I do not see why we should discriminate between dogs and cats. Both have walked the long roads of history with mankind. As for me, I do not feel a house is well-furnished without both dogs and cats, preferably at least two of each. And I am sorry for people who limit their lives by excluding either. I was fortunate to grow up with kittens and puppies and wish every child could have that experience.

Another mistake some people make is to believe generalizations about dogs and cats. They differ in individual personalities much as people themselves do. If you are fortunate enough to raise a litter of puppies or kittens, it is fascinating to watch them as they develop into separate persons. And every one, in his or her own way, gives you love and companionship and a kind of sharing which is often missing in human relationships.

Our black Manx, for instance, was not a lap sitter and cuddler. He was a big solid cat with sea-green eyes set in a blocky head. He had the high hindquarters and truncated tail characteristic of his breed. He was composed in manner. We called him our English country gentleman. He was out of doors a good deal, going about his career of catching mice and barn rats. As for intelligence, I have told the tale often of the day we watched him from the kitchen window as he stepped quietly along the border carrying a weed stalk.

"He can't be trying to make a nest," said Jill. "Has he lost his mind?"

Then he stopped and poked the stalk upright in the

soft earth, tiptoed back, and sat motionless. In a few minutes the weed stalk moved, and then he pounced and jumped back with a mole in his mouth. Obviously, as the mole got near the surface the weed trembled, and he was an easy target. Had I been alone in the house, no one would have believed this, but there were three spectators to testify.

He was not a bird catcher, he was a mouser. On cold nights he would sit closer to the open fire than any other cat we had, his green eyes half-closed, his paws folded. His dense ebony fur would get so hot it worried me. Then suddenly his ears would prick up at some sound we could not hear, and he would uncoil himself and dash to the door. If nobody hurried to open it, he rolled over and over and over. He never miaowed. He simply rolled. It always worked! When he was ready to come in, he clawed at the door, and if that did not work, he jumped to the knob and clawed at it.

Undemonstrative Tigger did have plenty of feeling under that restrained manner. During a time of sorrow, when I sat with my head in my hands, I felt a soft but firm push against my ankle, and a blunt ebony head rubbed against me back and forth and back and forth. When I picked him up, he even let me cry a little before he went away and began a thorough scrubbing. He said very plainly that he had comforted me, which indeed he had.

Esmé, my seal-point Siamese, on the other hand, was a passionate, demonstrative princess. She was extremely fond of Tigger but did consider him a peasant compared to herself. She was also devoted to Dark Honey, the queen of the cockers, and they slept together in the armchair by the fireplace, Esmé tucking her small self under Honey's ample chest. But she considered me her special property and had a way of sitting right on my typewriter when I tried to work until I stopped and cuddled her. When I went away to New York on business, she retired to the front bathroom and hid under the pipes by the big old tub. On my return she remained in seclusion for a time and then flew down the stairs and jumped up on my desk. She stood with legs braced, tail lashing and sapphire eyes glaring. She screamed, as only a Siamese—or possibly a bobcat—can. Finally she forgave me and flung herself on my chest, digging her claws in. The purr came later and the kisses from a sandpapery tongue. I am always reminded of these stormy episodes when I take Amber to Kim, our beloved veterinarian, for Amber manages a thin hiss as he looks her over. He says, "If only we could explain to them."

Esmé would accept no explanation. I abandoned her at intervals, and that was it.

Amber is not like either Tigger or Esmé. She is the smallest cat we have ever had, getting up to five pounds at most, and her apricot undercoat is like down. Her ears stand up perfectly straight and are the color of the inside of a pink seashell. Her eyes vary from topaz to pure gold, depending on the light. The iris is onyx. She is as feminine as Esmé but not as violent, unless some stranger tries to sweep her up, crying, "Oh, the beautiful pussycat!" Then she stiffens and hisses.

When I have to leave her, the last thing I see as I drive away is a sad, desperate face at the window. When I come back, she is at the door, ready to fly into my arms, start spreading her paws, and purr as loudly as she can—you barely hear it. If I am carrying groceries, she helps by getting inside every grocery bag to check everything. If I have packages from the post office, she tries to untie the string and claw the wrappers open.

But she never reproves me. And she knows the sound of our car motor, for if strange cars drive up, she hides. When I drive in, she welcomes me. Workmen in the house often say, "Amber knew it was you. She told me."

I explain to her where I am going and why and how long I shall be gone, and I notice when we are on Cape Cod, she starts for the wing if I say I am going out for several hours. The afternoon sun shines there. If I say I shall be right back, she settles on the sofa.

She is an explorer, which the other cats were not. Quite often I am already late for a party and cannot find her. She usually turns up in the back of a bureau drawer I left open or under the sink or in the china cupboard. Once she was inside the washing machine, which had been left open to air out. But she is the only cat I have had who comes when she is called if she can get out. I no longer leave bureau drawers closed after shutting her in a few times. Her miaow is so faint it isn't much good as an SOS.

Normally she is never more than a few feet away, so if I do not see her for twenty minutes, I look for her. She may be on the top shelf of the bookcases or tucked in among the Limoges tea set in the cabinet or dozing on the mantel or under my bedspread in a cozy nest. She is more airborne than the others; her motto "The higher the better." Even Esmé could not leap from the floor to the refrigerator top without one stop on the nearest counter.

She is also the only cat I have had who does not like

me to read. This means I am not concentrating on her, so she leaps onto the book or magazine, stretches out a paw, and claws the pages with great energy. It always works, for I feel reading isn't that important when a small person is lonely because I am off in Africa or back in the eighteenth century.

Amber has one serious problem—or, rather, I have. She was ill much of the time when she was first added to my life at six weeks. It was difficult to feed her because of various stomach and intestinal ailments. She grew to be strong and healthy, but food was a continuing battle. Having raised cockers and Irish setters and other cats, I was used to putting down a tasty dish of food and going about my business. I got used to feeding my delicate kitten with a teaspoon of junior baby food. Now she is six, she will usually eat directly from her bowl, providing the menu suits her, but often I sit at the counter holding a teaspoon. It tastes better, Amber says.

She is fond of asparagus tips, diced broiled beef or lamb or flounder filets. She will not eat flounder inland, however; she wants it on Cape Cod fresh from the sea water. She will not under any circumstances drink milk but savors light cream. If we have chili for supper, she waits for a chance to sneak a few mouthfuls, and she enjoys spaghetti sauce if she has a chance. Crisp morsels of bacon, snippets of cream cheese or mild cheddar are favorites, but Swiss she ignores. I always assumed she was the only cat who would sniff a fine dish of food and look up with disbelief, saying without words, "Do you expect me to eat this junk?" But one day I stood behind a man at the market who had half a basket of canned tuna fish and was explaining to the check-out girl that he had to return it because this was not the brand his cat liked best.

I began to buy some of the excellent cat foods for Blackberry, my daily boarder. Amber will dip her face in and eat some of it as I dish it out for Blackberry. But if I open a can and put it on her own tray, she ignores it. There is no monotony about our meals. Most of my closest friends care enough about her that, if we go out to eat, one will say, "I think I'll have fish tonight. Does Amber like broiled salmon, or should I order the halibut?" I go home with a kitty bag.

Sometimes she eats a fat fried shrimp or a spoonful of crabmeat, but never a clam or a snippet of broiled lobster. She is indifferent to chicken, whereas Esmé once landed on the shoulder of a guest who was standing by the fireplace eating a piece of fried chicken. Both Tigger and Esmé loved coddled eggs, but Amber will not touch an egg, coddled, beaten up raw, soft-boiled, hard-cooked, or with a hard-cooked yolk sieved.

She prefers to drink water dripping gently from a faucet or from the top of my water glass. Occasionally in the night she sips from her own porcelain French custard cup.

Each of our cats, even if hungry, always left one bite in their bowls. I recently read this is a cat habit, and I notice even the stray barn cats we feed leave exactly one morsel in their feeding dishes. This may be to ensure another bite later or to indicate they are decently fed. The barn cats come back in the night and finish off what they have left. Amber never does. If she gets hungry, she comes into my room and skips around, then starts to the kitchen and leaps to the counter where her tray is. But that leftover bit of supper is not touched.

One losing battle with her is that of medication. My friend Olive has a senior Siamese who needs pills several times a day, and Olive just pushes them in her mouth as a matter of course. Esmé, on occasion, would swallow a pill if needed when it was buried in a bit of tender baked chicken. Amber's tiny elegant lips freeze tight. When I pry them open and pop in a pill the size of a pinhead, I enjoy brief triumph but always find the pill later under my pillow or in her favorite chair. A pill beaten to a powder in the mortar and pestle and sprinkled over a favorite morsel fares no better. She *knows*! However, she dearly loves her vitamins, which come in a tube. All I have to say is that it is time for her vitamins, and she is on her counter waiting for me to open the tube and squeeze out a quarter of an inch for her to lick.

Our cockers and Irish setters usually had no feeding problems but did have their own preferences. Silver Moon loved tomato juice and had a small glassful daily. Sister was fond of vegetables except carrots. When I served them a beef stew simmered in the Dutch oven, she sorted out the carrots and laid them around the outside of her bowl. Holly, the setter, had a passion for ice cubes, and when she wanted one, sat by the refrigerator until the ice tray came out.

When she first began to be a regular visitor at Helen and Vicky's house on the Cape, they could not understand why she sat by the refrigerator but was not filled with enthusiasm at anything they took out to offer her. Finally one day they were about to have an afternoon drink, and when they took out the ice tray, Holly began to wag enthusiastically. She accepted an ice cube with joy and crunched it happily and came back for another. We never had another dog who wanted ice cubes.

Especially Me was one of eight, which is a large litter for
a cocker. We had to start supplementary feeding very
early. The other seven nursed in an ordinary manner
from the nipple of the bottle. Especially Me would not
open his mouth until I happened to turn him upside
down when I lifted him from the pen. Then he drank
the whole bottle. He lay in my hand waving his four
golden legs in the air and eating happily while his
mother sat complacently watching her first-born.

Our dogs and cats all had their own time sense
about when meals should be served. The Irish setter
preferred his main dinner when we had ours. Most of
the cockers wanted to eat earlier, possibly figuring that
then they would be ready for tidbits later. Tigger's
schedule varied according to when he came in from a
hunting expedition. When he was ready to eat, he sat by
the refrigerator and stared at the door. Then he moved
to the stove while his dinner was warmed up. Esmé ate
midmorning but asked for a little supper later on. Amber snacks, eating two or three teaspoonfuls at a time.
The experts who advise putting down the food and
then taking it up if it is not consumed would have to
adjust to her. Because of early stomach and intestinal
ailments, her capacity is limited. If her bowl happens to
be empty, she runs around and around in circles, and
if severely pressed, manages a faint miaow. We usually
eat supper together, and if she decides on a few more
bites of chop or steak, she stretches out one paw and pats
my arm. Sometimes late at night when I am in bed
watching Dick Cavett she wakes up, stretches, yawns
widely, and jumps on my chest, which means she would
like two teaspoons more of light cream. But she seldom

asks for food until I get up in the morning, whether it is early or late.

Some people do tell me dogs and cats are too much bother. We never found it so. When everything goes wrong with human relationships, which happens at times, there is comfort and restorative power in the soft muzzle laid gently on your lap, an ecstatic tail wagging, or a small head rubbing against your neck while a purr-song says, "How absolutely wonderful you are."

May in New England is the poetry of the seasons. After the bitter winter, roaring March, tentative April, May brings a time of blooming. Tender green leaves unfold. They look polished. As they thicken, the hills and valleys are bathed in a delicate green light. On the slope above the pond at Stillmeadow, the daffodils and narcissi Jill planted long ago star the grasses with gold and white. The wild violets make walking difficult. Who can bear to crush them?

Then there are the lilacs, amethyst and ivory clusters of blossoms which fill the air with sweetness. This is lilac countryside, and they still grow and bloom around the foundations of long-gone houses and along ancient stone walls. Their pointed leaves frame the flower heads with dark green. I like to pick a single leaf and feel the satiny texture. Connie and Alice and Anne bring in great bunches of our lilacs to put in old stoneware pitchers and grandmother's pewter coffeepot.

Toward the end of May, the phlox bursts forth. It seems to plant itself and grows like a weed. I like the pale lavender with white narcissi in a china pitcher my mother painted. (In the days of china painting, she did dinner sets, tea sets, and coffee sets.)

The few old apple trees in the upper orchard cloud the air with pink and white, and the morel mushrooms flourish around them. These are shaped like Christmas trees and have been called beefsteak mushrooms. They are spongy in texture and are big enough to be sliced lengthwise, broiled in butter, and served one mushroom to a person. Curt brought in one last weekend that was over four inches high as near as I could tell.

Rhubarb and asparagus provide special May treats. Rhubarb looks tropical, with the enormous emerald leaves. The stalks are light green and rosy pink and have a spicy tartness when cooked. We have always felt rhubarb pie was the queen of pies.

Now the birds begin to sing early in the morning, and the air is full of wings as they go about nest building. We usually have a robin who nests on a beam in the well-house roof, a nice cozy spot. One pair of cardinals has been around all winter, and I was fortunate enough to see Mr. Cardinal feeding his mate as she perched on a fence post. He kept poking tidbits down her open beak until she finally ruffled her wings and flew back to the nest.

A pair of mallard ducks has moved to the pond, and we hope they will raise their family there. There are no longer as many quiet ponds as there used to be in this countryside, and a good many rippling trout brooks have been polluted as developments move in, but our own pond is still a haven for wildlife.

This May, I saw a strange sight one dusk as I looked out. A plump raccoon came backing down the giant maple which is nearest my bedroom window. Paw by paw the coon moved, the hind legs lowered alternately, the forelegs clutching desperately. This tree is taller than the Stillmeadow rooftop, and it was a long, hard descent. I called Alice and Anne to watch, and when the coon made it to the ground and went toward the swamp, they ran out to put food in a convenient spot.

The next midday I saw the coon coming back to the tree carrying what looked like a bundle of fur. At first I thought it must be a young squirrel or rabbit, but as the coon began to carry it up the tree, I noticed the color of the fur—and it was neither. It was something I had never seen before, a baby raccoon. It did not struggle as the mother began the ascent. The climb was as perilous as any faced by a mountain climber and took a long time. Finally Mama reached the crotch of the tree—a point higher than the roof of the house. There the two vanished. I felt as if I myself had climbed Mount Everest and sat down to recover with a cup of coffee.

Some neighbors dropped in later for tea, and afterward I was busy dishing out dinner for the visiting barn cats. Finally I came back to my room to do a bit of typing and glanced out the window at the peach-colored afternoon sky.

And there across the grass came the coon with another burden clinging to her neck. The sense of determination with which she began that climb left me breathless with admiration. Up she went, paw by paw, holding her head up enough so the baby swung free of the rough bark. They vanished in the crotch.

Somehow she felt she must move her family to a spot safer than the one they were born in. And two were nested down in that crotch. I am sure she must have enlarged a knothole there, and the tree man would say this is bad for the tree, but I made her a solemn promise that she would be undisturbed. She would also get handouts as long as needed. I also prayed she would not venture from our protected acreage.

Even Jeremy Swamp Road is no longer safe for wildlife or house pets who happen to move out of their yards. Too many speeders gun their motors around the winding narrow road. Some motorcyles race on it. The horseback riders still use it but have to tighten the reins as the cyclists boom past. The overall passion today seems to be to get there faster.

Our favorite barn cat was Mittens. She was small, part tiger-colored but with white paws and a white collar. She had five toes like her mother and spent most of her time playing around the well house. Most of these barn cats come for food. They have made a narrow path across the lawn from the well house to the road and thence to the barn where our neighbor keeps his Black Angus. Two of the handsome males condescend to have a pat now and then. But if anyone comes to the path by the well, they vanish instantly. Even when their bowls of food are brought out, they are wary.

But Mittens wanted just one thing. She wanted to be a house cat and made it quite plain. She was a lap sitter and a purrer. She preferred sleeping on the wellhouse cover on an old bath rug to going to the barn at dusk.

When Amber was not in residence, Mittens came into the house to play with Alice and Anne. Every time the back door opened, her wistful face was turned to the kitchen. We hoped to find her a home she could rule over, but at her first heat, she mated and obviously planned to have her kittens in a warm burrow by the woodshed, where she herself was born.

But for some reason her kittens were born during the night somewhere else. I missed her at breakfast when I went to pour a saucer of light cream for her while Amber had hers. She had been run over at the edge of Jeremy Swamp Road beside our mailbox. A neighbor child came running with the news.

Mittens was on her way back to Stillmeadow carrying a small mouse and just could not make it fast enough to avoid the hit-and-run driver. Her back was broken.

Just a stray cat, the motorist would say. But I wonder what he did that was valuable in that half minute when he would not slow down?

As for us, the memory of a gentle person who spent her brief life giving love and accepting it will always be with us. It is true she did not actually belong to anybody —but Alice and Anne keep fresh flowers on her grave, and when I look out and see the other cats sitting by the well house, there is an empty space that none of them can fill.

I would like to see the day when car motors will have built-in controls regulating speed or better driver examinations will be given when licenses are applied for. Despite the fact that we live in a jet age, I believe we need to rethink our attitude toward the importance of speed and more speed.

When the Full Flower Moon shines, it is time for my unicorn to come down from the old apple orchard to the pond. He crops the wild violets as he steps delicately toward the cool, sweet water. Moonlight silvers his hoofs and horn. He comes only in May, and I am the only one who has seen him, although Anne spends many evenings watching for him, and I believe one day she too will become his friend.

I have described this magical experience often. I first met him long ago when I went out for a brief escape from a difficult day. My heart was heavy. I walked up the slope, stepping on the wild white violets that grow so thickly there, stopping now and then to gather a bunch of them. The air smelled of dusk and dew, and the pond was dipped in moonlight. There is always a special time in May between twilight and night as if the dying day stretched a hand out to the darkness.

And there he came, moving soundlessly from the woods. His slender body was white as first snow, his single horn silver. He cropped the violets as he went. I stood trying not to breathe, but my bouquet trembled in my hands, and he realized I was there and lifted his head. We looked at each other. Then deliberately he lipped a mouthful of violets and continued to the pond. The tip of his horn sent small ripples out as he dipped his head to drink.

Finally I spoke in a small voice. "Welcome," I said. "Do not forsake me."

Then he was gone. I went back to the house, feeling strong enough to face any crisis. It was a long time before I mentioned him to anyone, but eventually the family learned about him and accepted him with good grace. He became known as Mama's unicorn, and often in violet time they asked, "Has he come yet?"

Of all legendary creatures, the unicorn seems to be most mysterious. There is one story that he was the only animal left out of the ark. The reason was that he had no mate, and the ark passengers went in two by two. A later legend says that only pure maidens could approach him, and some early paintings do depict a maiden near him. A third belief at one time was that to look upon the unicorn was fatal. All the early writings about him agree that he is never to be tamed or harnessed or pull burdens and that he moves like lightning.

There is a famous tapestry in the Cloisters in New York City of a unicorn hunt, with the last panel showing him captured and bleeding inside a rosy circular paling. He has a grave, aloof look even with blood staining his snowy coat, and one gets the feeling that none of this has any import. I used to go to the Cloisters whenever I could, and eventually I was fortunate enough to be able to buy a copy of this section of the tapestry, which I framed to hang in the keeping room above the ancient pine commode. The whole background is strewn with exquisite blossoms in glowing colors and the effect is one of strange tranquillity.

It is the only picture hanging in the narrow room.

I have had many happy moments dreaming of my unicorn, and I believe happiness is simply reaching out for something lovely and believing in it. Even on a January night when snow drifts deep and the wind is lonely, I look toward the frozen pond and remember that violets will bloom again and my unicorn will walk on them, strange and beautiful and steeped in silver.

All of us need some magic in our lives, and all we have to do is believe in it.

As I write, we have had a new happening as Anne calls it. Our county was put on a tornado watch. The children had gone back to New York, and Amber and I were alone. I listened to the radio warnings and the directions for getting ready. Then I sat down with Amber on my lap and wondered what to do. It had rained for more than a week (breaking all records for May), so the doors were swollen and only one outside door would open at all. The one back door which still swung if I kicked it would naturally be in the wrong direction for escape as it opens toward the old well house. The well house is picturesque and covered with a thirty-year growth of wisteria but would certainly be flattened in a jiffy by even a modest tornado. I could imagine Amber and me buried in old beams and wisteria trunks.

There was not, I decided, an inner room to hide in. The house is built around the fourteen-foot hand-hewn stone chimney with the rooms fanning out to the outer walls. The only inner protected area is the great fireplace itself, the heart of the farmhouse. Amber and I could climb in there—Cinderellas in the ashes—but not for long, since I would have to crouch. I considered the cellar, but the stairs down are really a ladder, and I cannot negotiate them since my knees are now unwilling to bend. My knees also ruled out getting under the great rope bed in my room. (It now has a modern box spring and mattress but still has not much space underneath except for puppies or kittens. It is even difficult to get the vacuum cleaner under it.)

Amber presented a problem in any case, because she is averse to being swooped up and lugged around from one place to another. She prefers to follow my foosteps so closely I am careful not to step on her.

In the end we spent the last hour of the tornado watch in the relative security of my bed, where I tried to

read Katherine Mansfield's letters once more. And when this particular tornado hit New Jersey, I felt I really knew what so many have gone through when a tornado watch is announced. We have been through a good many hurricanes, but I think tornadoes bring a greater sense of helplessness and hopelessness, perhaps second only to earthquakes.

A minor crisis occurred at Stillmeadow on a peaceful, sunlit day this week. I had worked all morning and went out to fix some lunch while I listened to my favorite country music on the radio. I was humming "The Green Grass of Summer" when I looked into the back kitchen and saw a cat. My first thought was that Amber could not have gained six pounds since breakfast, and then the cat turned to look at me, and it was definitely not Amber's delicately boned head. It was the biggest male of our boarders. The next instant I saw Amber on the top shelf of the cupboard, coiling herself up for a spring at the invader.

Somehow these crises always come when I am alone. What had happened was obvious. The cat was hungry and I had ignored him, so he tore out the bottom screen of the back door and came in. I could hear him saying, "Oh, you think I am not a house cat, do you?"

My voice came out in a croak as I ordered Amber to *stay*, which she normally obeys. Meanwhile I grabbed the dish of food from the counter while the visitor flew around in circles.

"I'm getting it—I'm getting it—just come out—" I kept saying, and miraculously he believed me and spun to the door. Amber was frozen on the shelf, and I got out with the food as fast as the big boy, who switched his tail and jumped through the torn screen.

I made a sign and taped it to the inner wooden door saying, "Cat broke screen. Keep door closed."

Then I heated a bowl of soup and spilled some on the counter and had to mop it up. Now it might have been the two would have made their own diplomatic agreement. However, I know how jealous Amber is. And I also know she will attack anything up to full-grown raccoons if possible, but she has only one tooth or two since she had surgery for a jaw infection. She also has regular manicures when her claws begin to turn in and are uncomfortable. So her only weapon is her fierce, indomitable spirit.

I also knew this particular male has a habit of cuffing the other cats away from the food dishes, snarling and screeching until he gets the cream of the meal. He is twice Amber's size, muscular and tough from coming up the hard way.

And finally and most fatal, I knew the dish on the counter had liver bits in it, and although liver does not agree with Amber, she loves it passionately. So does the boarder.

I decided when my heart began to beat reasonably that this beautiful male would be easy to adopt. Although he is the wildest of all our barn cats, he was brave enough to rip out the screen and get *in the house* to locate the dinner he felt was overdue. It would not take long to persuade him to move into the house and sit by the fire polishing himself on winter evenings, instead of living in George's drafty barn in a nest of hay. He might even condescend to sit on a lap to have his ears rubbed. I said as much to Amber and asked her if one more cat wouldn't be company for her when I have to go out.

Amber's reply was to switch her tail, give a final hiss toward the back door, and wash away the memory with a good bath. Then she got on my lap and pawed away my book, kneaded her raspberry-tipped paws on me, purred her loudest purr. All I want is you, said she firmly.

So all I must do is get new screening on the back door and be sure to feed the visitor *on time!*

In May 1973 Southbury was three hundred years old. It was settled by a small band of determined men and women who came in boats which they paddled along the river. They had the usual difficulties—bad weather, insufficient food, and only a vague idea of their destination. They had a grant of land but no guide to it. Fortunately, the Indians were friendly in this area.

Finally they reached their goal, landed, and gathered under a great white oak to kneel and pray for God's blessing. Like most of the New England settlers, they came to establish their own church and worship God in their own way. It was fairly common for schisms to develop in church groups, whereupon some members broke away and moved. Just how basic the differences were one cannot know, but they could probably have been settled amicably except for the violent emotions these schisms caused.

These particular settlers found a fertile valley overlooked by rolling green hills. The Pomperaug River flowed clear and sweet, and there were many streams filled with fish. Game was plentiful; the soil was rich and dark. It was not easy to till because the glacier that moved down from Maine in the beginning left great boulders and smaller rocks, which had to be dug out by hand in order to clear fields.

There were a few Indian villages and scattered corn patches, but the Indians were chiefly hunters and fishers and left most of the wilderness as it was, beautiful, lonely. But the white man began to farm and to build. Trees fell, brush fires burned, boulders were moved. Boundaries between farms were marked by fences built of the great rocks. Some of these still remain, including those surrounding Stillmeadow. Some were hauled away during the machine age for foundations and river dams, and some were taken by travelers who wanted rock gardens.

The early houses usually had cellars with walls of hand-hewn granite. Stillmeadow has stone fireplaces and hearths, and the well is lined with stone. When you step out of the doors, you walk on immense stone steps. The most spectacular boulder rises at one end of the pond, as tall as Anne and as immovable as it has been for centuries. I love to walk down to the pond and look at it, for it reminds me of nature's strength and of the old hymn "Rock of Ages, Cleft for Me."

Every rock is a history, as my father said. He was a geologist and used to take me to hunt for and study rocks. He could find the glacial furrows on them, describe what minerals they contained, figure out their origin, and make me live in the Ice Age even on a steamy August day.

A friend once said to me, "If only your father had loved people as he loved rocks!" And I realized it was true. He was impatient with people and always expected them to conform to his ideas. Nobody except my mother was without flaw, and even she had failings, such as not wanting to bound up every morning at six and liking to sit down in the afternoon for tea and watercress sandwiches (a waste of time, he said). But rocks were without flaw. His office was full of special ones, rosy or gray or striated with green. I used to go in and feel them when he was out in the yard murdering the lawn mower by running it too fast.

I am sure the early settlers loved them, too, no matter how difficult they were to move and hew, because those used for hearths and chimney walls are always sparkling with bits of minerals that blend with one another. I do not think this is accidental; I think the stonemasons chose them.

Now in Southbury the bulldozers are at work. Ancient stone walls vanish overnight. Asphalt paving overlays old meadows where wild flowers grew. A settler from three hundred years ago would be lost. The old houses with hand-cut clapboards are fewer every year, and the saddler's shop has been replaced by a gas station. We even have traffic lights, although there are still, I am glad to say, no sidewalks.

But as the tercentenary was celebrated, I found something had survived the modern age. And this has to do with people. There is still a belief in most of the villagers that Southbury is important, that it has values worth preserving. Aside from a few who wish to exploit the area, most still have a love of the land and honesty in their relationships with one another. For the tercentenary the men grew beards, and the women wore bonnets and many-petticoated costumes and were very uncomfortable. It seemed rather like a carnival at times.

But even the various spectaculars and fireworks and parachute jumping and the five-hundred-pound ice cream cone could not change Southbury into an amusement park. When the bunting came down and the beards vanished and women climbed out of the tiers of uncomfortable petticoats and hung up their bonnets, the village was itself again. It was comfortable and familiar. Friends had time to visit at the market, neighbors dropped in wearing jeans and sweat shirts. Talk turned to the next town meeting and the tax rate. In a way, I felt we came home.

What the next hundred years will bring is not predictable. But I hope the basic personality of our town may survive, with some woodlands and meadows left, some streams still rippling with trout, some winding country roads (unpaved). And a few farmers still harvesting the sweet hay in season and milking plump cows at sunset. I hope that there will be room for gardens and that the wild roses will climb the old stone fences and children can still pick wild strawberries in June.

This is the heritage I wish for this three-hundred-year-old community, not that it should become just another industrial center crammed with factories, condominiums, high-rise buildings, and with planes jetting above the smog. I hope that it still may provide quiet country living for children to come.

By the end of May the iris blooms, lemon yellow and amethyst. The wild iris, which we call flags, open deep purple blossoms around the pond. Sweet phlox is

in blossom, pink-lavender. There are masses of it all
around Stillmeadow, growing tall and wild, not like the
low phlox in gardens. When I look out of the window,
drifts of it rise against the emerald-green foliage of low
bushes and giant ferns.

Olive and I walked down to the pond at sunset
yesterday, stopping to pull an armload of rhubarb and
pick the pale iris. The pond was dark and still, but the
sky over the old orchard was lighted with a glow like a
ripe peach. I pointed out the path of my unicorn but
explained he had gone with the violets. A single bird
note and the sound of the brook running into the pond
broke the quietude.

When we came back, it was cool enough to light
the fire, and I wrote her a little verse before supper.

For Olive

What is time?
It is a moment when we walk to the pond
Over the green grass
Past sweet phlox purple in the dusk
And rhubarb, rosy-stalked along the path
To the water, dark and satin-smooth beyond.
Was this a moment of eternity?
Or a memory fragmentary?
Or only a piece of today
Folded away?

SUMMER

There used to be a time when great friendships were taken for granted. David and Jonathan were famous, and in later times history records many deep devotions such as Hamlet and Horatio (who were not fictional, I am sure). In the great days of England there were Keats and his Severn. It was not a matter of sex, for it was also usual for gentlewomen to have such close friendships that they wrote to one another constantly if they were separated for a while, and often if a friend was in trouble, she was simply invited to move in and be taken care of even if the household was brimming with children, aunts and uncles, or husband's kin.

It was not unusual for deep friendships to bloom between men and women, all involving a great deal of correspondence. Times were more leisurely then, and society had a different texture from ours.

Today as I read books and magazines I find a massive output of writing that consists of sex relationships, sex problems, and how to fulfill one's life by sex. A minor output considers parent-child problems and occasionally some adventurous author explains to the harried housewife how to run her house.

133

But I think a good deal myself about the importance of friendship, for I believe close friendships have
an inestimable value in life, and I begin to have an
anxiety lest eventually nobody will know the meaning
of them. I grew up in a small town where Father was a
college professor, and those colleagues he did not de-
spise often became his intimate friends. And our big
living room was a haven for Mama's best friends who
brought all their troubles to her. There were couples,
too, who were with us on camping trips, picnics, and
Sunday afternoon rides. None of us would ever forget
the trip to the Dells with the Russells when they had
five flat tires and Papa's radiator boiled over. (So did he).

As for me, I had a best, *best* friend to whom I confided everything, including my desperate love for the
football left end. I had a number of others to whom I
was deeply devoted, about evenly divided between the
girls and the boys. Friends were forever loyal and were
expected to be. The worst sin one could commit was to
be untrue to a friend, and a few who lacked faithfulness
were ostracized rather soon.

Now I try to analyze the change in our lives today.
I think as a people we are sociable; in fact, I know a
good many men and women who seem frightened to be
alone but need the protection of a group most of the
time. However cocktail parties, "open house," buffets,
barbecues, and dinner parties may ease our insecurity,
they cannot substitute for a walk in the sun with a close
friend or an evening by the fire with two or three whom
we love.

For who can be close to anyone in a gathering with
twenty or thirty people milling around, outtalking one

another and never having a chance to say anything? Occasionally I meet someone at a cocktail party and have just time enough to feel I want this person for a friend, and if I am fortunate, he or she suggests it is a mutual experience. But, then, I can meet some stranger at the post office and feel a kinship immediately.

Possibly the rise of the cocktail age has something to do with fewer true friendships; I don't know. Or possibly it is also because this is a competitive society, with every man battling for himself. Exchanging confidences can be dangerous—if you make a mistake. The McCarthy persecutions instituted a time of terror, when even expressing an opinion could be ruinous, and there are moments when I think we are coming to that again.

The Vietnam war has been blamed for many things, and I suspect it had something to do with personal isolation, too, for we now tend to keep conversation superficial in case that other person does not agree with our policy. We keep our cool, as we say, by talking about the weather. I do not know what we would do without the weather, and sometimes I imagine all of us in some balmy climate where it never changes. What would we find to discuss? Would we sink into a tropical silence?

Aside from the weather, the only reasonably safe topic is television—and that can be hazardous when a program someone just adores is defined as complete rot by someone else. Then it is best to go back to the barometer reading.

This has nothing to do with real friendship, of course. A close, warm friendship is as rugged as a fishing boat going out to the wild sea on a dark day when the tide is high. My own dearest friends do not agree with me on many things, but we can talk about anything and argue and argue, and there is benefit for both sides. For at the core of this relationship is a community of feeling which is basic and has nothing to do with disagreements about politics, going to the moon, or whether we need a new development in the middle of town.

We love and trust a true friend for what he or she is, and living is more enriched by the relationship than words can express. There is in each of us, I think, a deep loneliness, and friendship eases it immeasurably. How sad to think it is growing so scarce nowadays when we need it most.

What does a friendship really mean? In my list, trust, loyalty, and sharing. These are big responsibilities but well worth it. You may tell a true friend anything you wish and be assured it won't be repeated all over town. If you make an unwise remark, it is a stone dropped in a well. The next day someone will *not* call up and say, "I hear you said so and so."

It means your friend is loyal to the relationship and not what used to be called "a summer friend," who faded with the first frost. It also means sharing. It means you are grateful for the privilege of sharing the hard times as well as the glorious ones. If your friend turns to you in trouble, you are really a friend and feel you are worth something special in this troubled world.

There is a special happiness, too, about friends you do not lose by time or distance. Some of them you may hear from only at Christmas, but the tie is as strong as ever and is one of the brightest aspects of the holiday season. Others may be new friends, and when they come into your life, you feel both an excitement and a sorrow for all the days you missed knowing them.

I would like to feel that friendship will survive as long as mankind inhabits this planet. Sometimes someone says to me, "I don't want to get involved." Or, "I mind my own business and don't depend on anyone." Or, "I am not going to lose my freedom."

This may sound strong and, in a way, noble, but think about the words. We are all involved with one another, whether we accept it or not. We are all born, we all die. We suffer illness. None of us really escapes insecurity at times. We are capable of happiness and love and of loss and longing. We cannot really isolate ourselves from our fellow human beings. Even the few individualists like Howard Hughes cannot escape entanglements with society some time or other.

The old words "No man is an island" are still true.

Therefore, abiding, deep relationships may bring an ease to the heart as we pursue our common destiny. Delights we can share are richer, sorrows lessened, fears diminished. Marriages in which husband and wife are firm friends seem impregnable, and I am sorry the sex experts ignore this.

Most of those marriages I have seen fail have one thing in common: The partners lack the quality of friendship. Trust and loyalty and old-fashioned good will could save many that I am familiar with. When a wife says to me gaily, "Of course I wouldn't trust Henry around the corner," I begin to wonder. And when the husband says, over his drink, "Well, you have to watch Emily," I think both of them unconsciously do mean it.

Now back a minute to summer friendships. They bloom like roses and like roses fade too soon. Winter friendships are more important, for they withstand the harsh winds of January and the icy fall of sleet. They are what we all need and are as warming as a fire on the hearth on a winter night.

Sometimes I am asked how to make friends. "I just don't have any real friends," writes a lonely woman or man. "Why don't I have any? What is wrong? What can I do?"

There are always slick answers by suave experts, but I doubt whether they solve much. As far as I have known, the one way to establish deep friendships is to reach out with understanding and sympathy and a strong intent to share. This involves a considerable amount of listening—and listening is almost a forgotten art in these troubled times. It involves thinking about the other person instead of concentrating on oneself. Often it is not easy, but most valuable experiences are not. It may involve patience and always means appreciating the friend to the fullest degree.

The natural community of being which is part of friendship must be nourished, and one quick and easy way to destroy this is to criticize. When someone begins a sentence, "I know you won't like to hear this but—," or, "I feel I must say this to you," the waters are already troubled. Sound criticism seldom begins this way but is more likely to begin, "I know how it is and I share it with you. The only thing I wonder is—"

I would like to think friendship is worth working at all our lives long.

Trust, loyalty, sharing—what do they really mean? We live in an age of such elegant-sounding words uttered by politicians and nations' representatives. We hear endless speeches and countless extravagances in television speeches and commercials. Sometimes I feel like one of my Cape Cod sea gulls sitting on the edge of Mill Pond polishing away the excess moisture on his body with an energetic beak. I tend to distrust or not listen to any word which is not specific and definite, and I believe a great many people feel as I do.

So I spend considerable time explaining to myself and to Amber that trust is not a surface word but means something vital. There is no trust between nations, none between political parties (the Watergate incident is a prime example), very little between religious groups (Ireland is the most tragic evidence of this).

Even in our personal lives we have begun to realize we must be careful about having faith in our own social groups and be certain we are not betrayed in an unguarded moment. Most people can think of dozens of instances when they wish they had not confided in a supposed friend. I always remember a day in August when I drove to a tea party with a companion. It was over 90 degrees, and the affair was a casual gathering. On the way, I said that I hated the idea of going out that day and wished I were at home in comfortable clothes. Some time later it was reported to me that everyone now knew I was unsociable and did not like going out and just wanted to be left alone. I lived this down and, while doing so, learned a lesson.

A good many remarks taken out of context can cause trouble, but who wants to monitor every sentence day and night? What we all want is freedom to express what we wish to those we can trust.

Loyalty can be a deep and abiding joy, and I fear it is getting rather rare. It means you defend what you believe in and those you believe in and that you are faithful in fair times and in bitter times. We speak of it most often in connection with our governments, our flags, our presiding officials, and our particular religions. It involves, to me, a sturdiness of spirit and a gentleness of heart beyond any price. It is not blind, unthinking acceptance but rather an appreciation of the best and a willingness to work toward it. Most of us felt the end of the McCarthy era was final, but it wasn't. Some of the most loyal Americans have been punished during this decade for loyalty to our country, and it is a pity the government could not realize it.

Loyalty to our personal friends also does not mean we find them perfect. But we do not betray their weaknesses, and this comes down to the problem of gossip. We all know a few people who cannot wait to report anything adverse about anyone in the neighborhood or village or township. I myself take such a violent view of this that I refuse to listen. And I do not repeat the gossip which can sometimes destroy an innocent person. "I heard that—" can be deadly as a bomb and fall with the same result.

Sharing is the final test of true friendship. All of us wish to avoid suffering, but we all experience it in this unquiet world. Sharing eases grief, adds luster to joys, and always increases our feeling of being needed. I think the saddest words in the world are, "Nobody needs me any more."

I hope deep friendships will become less rare in our time, especially since this world has become so impersonal, so much a matter of computers and ratings and machinery. We are not Social Security numbers; we are all individuals, no two alike, every one a whole being needing to experience real relationships and to have the blessing of mutual trust and friendship as we make our common journey through life.

As the roses bloom in summer, we fill Stillmeadow with them, in my grandmother's old silver teapot or the moss-rose sugar bowl or a milk-glass spooner. Roses are delicate in texture and should not be put into heavy containers, I think. If you bring them in from your own garden, it is well to immerse them in lukewarm water to their necks for a time to absorb all the moisture they can. I have excellent luck with florist roses in winter by soaking them like this overnight. Then cut the stems on a slant and arrange the flowers so they are *not* crowded. They want room to breathe, just as we do.

An uneven number of blooms looks better, and all the blooms should not be the same height. Always have one or two near the lip of the container, which gives a solid relationship to your bouquet. If the foliage is too thick, snip off a few leaves. At night I always put my roses to bed by moving them to a cool room (we use our back kitchen for this) and adding fresh cool water. Occasionally a rose will droop and decide not to open, and sometimes dipping the stem in very hot water helps this. Florist roses are apt to have this fault.

None of us like to see the delicate petals fall, and with a little patience it is possible to keep their fragrance to bring summer memories into January. Potpourri is simply dried flower petals mixed with herbs and spices. It was used in the very early sixteenth century by queens and princesses—partly, we have to admit, because with the lack of sanitation and plumbing the ancient castles were anything but sweet-smelling. Ladies carried jeweled perforated boxes with the dried petals most of the time, kept silver bowls of them in their boudoirs, and also sprinkled them in the bed linens.

There are many recipes for potpourri in old cookbooks or in libraries. But the basic method is the same. Salt the petals a little and spread on a screen to dry. Store them in covered jars until you make your potpourri. If you have lavender, you are especially fortunate, and if you can get orris root, it is a help.

To make the potpourri, you mix the dried flower petals with herbs such as rosemary, thyme, mint, marjoram, and parsley, and add spices to your own taste. We like plenty of cinnamon and cloves, allspice, coriander, mace, and cardamom. You use 1 cup of herbs to 1 quart of dried petals. Salt lightly the bottom of a jar and alternate layers of petals and herbs. Tuck in a few whole blossoms, seal the jar, and let rest for about a month. Then use it wherever you wish.

Sometimes you may be able to get oil of lavender, but use whatever perfume you have and you will have fragrance that is delightful. You may use almost any flowers except the strongly scented ones like calendulas or marigolds.

If you are handy with a needle, you may make little mesh or cheesecloth packets to tuck in your linen drawers or hang in the closets. If not, you can sprinkle a little in the bottom of drawers and on shelves.

My granddaughter Anne, at eleven, has developed a great gift for potpourri-making and invents her own combinations, and they are delightful. She uses an old window screen for the drying, but a stretched cheesecloth will do very well.

Incidentally, for people who must travel a good deal, a bag of potpourri in the suitcase brings a fresh touch to hotel rooms, airports, and railroad stations.

Another easy freshener can be made at any season. Anne makes these clove oranges to hang in closets and tucks them in our stockings at Christmas. Simply take a good orange (or lemon) and stick cloves in it all over, as many as you can possibly poke in. Then tie a ribbon around the whole fruit and hang it from a hanger in the closet. The spicy odor is a treat. As the fruit dries, it becomes more fragrant, and it lasts a long time.

Days may be hot in summer in our part of New England, windless and burning, but nights usually are not, although from mid-July to August the thermometer climbs to incredible heights. It is called corn-growing weather, and so it is, and the musky smell of ripening corn is surely unforgettable. We planted most of the upper meadow in corn when we first came to Stillmeadow, dreaming of corn roasts, corn soufflés, corn pudding, corn relish, and corn chowders. But the raccoons had their own plans and ate half the crop before it was ready to pick. A coon uses his paws like hands and strips the ears neatly and gobbles the golden rich kernels in the night. We still had enough for ourselves the first few seasons and then gave up and planted corn only in the area by the back door. We put potatoes and squash in the upper field. And we had enough of both to start a market.

Once you have picked your own corn and rushed to the house with it and shucked it and dropped it in already boiling water, something new has come into your life. For corn is a very perishable vegetable and loses the sweet milky juice rapidly. Some of the roadside

stands advertise that theirs is picked at four in the
morning and rushed in and is *fresh,* but it is not the
same.

My earliest memories of what corn can be were
when Mama and I spent summers at Grandfather's farm
in Massachusetts. My cousins and I were not supposed to
play in the cornfields, so of course we did, and the corn
was tall above our heads. Sometimes we helped the delightful Irish cook shuck it when it was picked, and
since there might be eight or nine at the dinner table,
there was a wash basket full of corn husks.

Later on when Father gave up the wandering life
of a mining engineer and we settled down in a house in
Wisconsin, he used to take me to hunt Indian arrows
and pottery shards in cornfields at nearby farms. The
rich earth between the rows was full of treasures. My
only problem was that I could not keep up with Father,
and his leaping figure would simply vanish. I used to
feel humiliated, but later I realized nobody ever kept
up with Papa. I heard from a former student of his who
had taken geology at Lawrence that she would never
forget the field trips because they nearly killed everyone.

I am told that corn is so ancient no historian can
trace its beginning. The American Indians cultivated it,
but it evidently dates farther back into unknown periods. In Truro, on Cape Cod, there is Corn Hill, which
summer tourists visit, and the story is that the Pilgrims
discovered a cache of corn buried on that hill by notic-
ing the earth was freshly dug. With their usual morality,
they dug down and carried it all off.

It was called maize in early times, and what we call
corn meal was Indian meal. Corn-meal mush was a staple
in our forefathers' households. And oddly enough, pop-

corn was raised by the Indians, as well as what we now call field corn. I would like to know who tasted the first true sweet corn. When we first planted ours, we had several rows of what was called the blue Mexican corn, which was my favorite—perhaps because of the dark-blue streaked ears. They were small and tightly kerneled and not as juicy but had a nutty flavor.

A Stillmeadow specialty has always been Connecticut Corn Pudding. When corn is in season and we have had enough of it boiled or roasted or in corn chowder, we make it as follows:

Broil or fry until crisp 6 strips of bacon, and drain on a paper towel. In the drippings (2 tablespoons), sauté ½ diced green pepper and 1 small onion, diced. To this add 2 cups corn (frozen or canned if you have no fresh), ½ cup soft bread crumbs, 2 eggs, beaten, 2 cups top milk, and the bacon. Season to taste with seasoned salt and seasoned pepper. Stir together and pour into a greased 1½ quart casserole. Top with ½ cup buttered crumbs and bake at 375 degrees for about 40 minutes. Serves six, presumably.

For a party supper, serve with paper-thin sliced ham and a tossed salad.

One final note about corn if you have to buy it at a market or at a roadside stand. I have often watched customers battling for the biggest, fattest ears, and then I choose the smallest ones, which are always more tender. I try to select ears which have moist husks, not burned-looking and dry. When I cook it, I add top milk and butter to the pot and a spoonful or so of sugar with the salt. This makes a fair substitute for the vanished milk sugar in the kernels.

I am always careful to watch the pot and not overcook the bought corn, for it toughens readily. When my ancient two-tined fork just pierces a kernel without too much struggle, I turn the heat off, let the corn rest a minute or so, and then serve with added butter on each ear.

If you save the husks and dry them well, they are fine for the fireplace, so corn is indeed a good friend to the homemaker. I have never slept on a corn-husk mattress, but a great many people did in the early days if they did not have featherbeds. You may also dry the whole ears, but if you hang them in a sheaf for harvest decoration by the front door, the birds will soon strip them—the bluejays, in particular, love them. I once got up at dawn because I heard banging on the Dutch door, and when I peeked out, I saw the flash of brilliant blue wings as the bluejays swooped and dined on my decorative effort.

The more I think about sweet corn, the more I wish I could know who first ate it, when it evolved from some wild grass somewhere in the haze of history. And I am sure it was first cooked when some careless person dropped some in the firepit and pulled it out and decided to peel back the charred husk and take a tentative bite. And then some brave soul figured out that pounding the kernels between two flat stones made a golden meal which would become a staple for generations to come.

Midsummer brings the thunderstorms to New England, and they have a grandeur which is awesome. When I was a small child, my father used to make me go out to watch the sky and enjoy the lightning, but that was one thing Papa never managed to teach me. Papa loved thunder and lightning, and I now think they released some pent-up emotions in him which he could not express. I did learn that the flashes you see and the bombing sounds you hear mean that you are still safe, but I always begged to go back into the house where Mama was pursuing her regular routine. I remember that even Papa could not get her out in the middle of a bad thunderstorm, because she always had something in the house that had to be done, but she never said she also hated the storms.

Weather reports do not matter. My cockers and Irish setters always knew when one was coming, and now Amber begins to lash her tail and move from room to room restlessly, even if the sky is serene and no clouds are visible. I feel the storms, too—it is rather like an electric current in the air and I feel tense and nervous.

In our valley a giant thunderstorm can come up almost instantaneously, because this is hill country, and the inky clouds may be hidden until the last moment. It is usually very still and hot, almost tropical. Then Amber flies to my bed as the first big drops fall and daylight diminishes. A premonitory roll of thunder comes, followed by jagged lightning in the sky over Jeremy Swamp.

My routine never varies. I turn on the lights and also get out the candles, for often the lightning takes out the transistors or whatever they are. I shut all the windows, which is a real problem in a 1690 house, for each one takes a dim view of being either closed or opened. There are several that I have to take a hammer to.

If it is late afternoon, I get out cold ham and salad

greens from the refrigerator, so if the electricity goes off I need not open the door, and I make a big pot of fresh coffee. As a last chore, I bring in all the feeding dishes by the old well house and fill them with the next banquet for the barn cats and coons. I leave them by the back door so I can pop them out as soon as the storm is over.

Jill used to rush to her garden and pick whatever was ripe. She always said Stillmeadow was a nest for thunderstorms and hurricanes, and it has certainly always been a favorite spot for both.

After a few summers we cabled the giant sugar maples that surround the house with copper cables and put extra lightning rods on house and barn. Even so, during one July thunderstorm I was on the way to the front living room when a ball of lightning came in and ran down the ruffled curtains, leaped to the fireplace, and exploded on the hearth. Oddly enough, the white sheer curtains were not even singed. But it took me some time to breathe naturally again.

Occasionally in our valley, barns are struck and do burn down, especially if there is hay in them, for apparently the moisture in the hay draws the lightning. And sometimes there are casualties because people will seek shelter under a nice big tree if they are caught outside. The last place in the world to be in a bad thunderstorm is under a big tree.

I can always tell if it is to be a bad storm, for the birds announce it. Suddenly you would not know there was a bird in Connecticut; some instinct warns them as it does Amber. They begin by flying around in circles, dipping and swooping. Then they vanish, as do the dozen squirrels. When the storm is really over, they are all back before the last rumble of thunder dies down.

In fact, one day I was sitting happily at my neighbors', having tea and watercress sandwiches, when I looked out of the window and put my plate down.

"I'd better get home," I told Steve and Olive. "There's a bad one coming."

"What do you mean?" asked Olive. "The weather report says clear for the weekend."

"I saw your birds," I said.

By the time I got back to Stillmeadow, the first lightning etched the sky, and we had a record-breaking thunderstorm. And when I got in the house, some of the cockers were already under my bed and the cats buried in the afghan on the couch.

Fortunately, thunderstorms do not last as long as hurricanes; and when they are over, the world is dazzling. The rain has such power that it polishes every dusty leaf, and every blade of grass is jeweled. The brook sends special music as she plunges down the hill to the pond, for she is brimming with almost as much water as when snow melt in spring feeds her. The whole hot summer earth is replenished, and looking out at the swamp, I see a cool mist rising as the stagnant water cools.

"Well, it cleared the air," says my dear friend George at the market. And I cannot help but think that all of us have personal thunderstorms in our lives, and perhaps they are sometimes able to clear the air too. I remember one dear friend who struggled patiently through more personal difficulties than I could ever describe, and one day when she came over, she said, "I simply exploded, Gladys! I don't know what came over me, but I just said everything right out. And somehow things are better now—I can't see why."

And I said, "After a thunderstorm the air is so clear and gentle, maybe that happened to you."

July and August bring the great tide of tourists to New England, and it ebbs only after Labor Day. We are a traveling nation, and I think we always have been since the days the Pilgrims left their homeland for uncharted wilderness in an undiscovered country. Now we have finally traveled to the moon, which as a simple country woman I feel dubious about. (I really do not like to look at the glorious, mysterious moon and picture the debris we have already left on her, including a golf ball.)

Seeking for gold, men, women, and children left their farms or villages and died, leaving their bones to mark the trails to the West. I do not read of many who turned back; most of them went on until they starved. They were foolhardy, for most of them started out with no equipment, no plan, no adequate food, only a dream. The few who made it found no Shangri-La, only more struggle to survive in an alien country. They are now chiefly remembered in history books, but they did, after all, open the West so that future generations could settle there and prosper.

I think of them when I see the endless stream of cars on the roads in midsummer. For nowadays we may go anywhere in this vast land on throughways marked with so many signs it is hard to read them all. We also carry maps from our filling stations and travel guides advertising stopping places from camp sites to motels and lodges. We are still, most of us, looking for that golden place, but now it is the perfect vacation spot we seek, and, alas, when we find it, we usually ruin it.

And this makes me think a great deal about people, summer people. Last summer when I was on Cape Cod, I was told 30,000 tourists came to the narrow land, and, as always, some Cape Codders predicted the whole Cape would sink right down into the sea just from the weight of their cars.

Most of those who come to Connecticut or Massachusetts are thoughtful, gentle people we are proud to meet. They are usually families with young children and a dog or two they would never leave behind, or a couple of cats. They come from California, Florida, Ohio, Minnesota, Oregon, and they appreciate everything about New England that is different. (I remember one man who said to me with awe, "I never saw an old house before.")

They visit historic monuments and take endless color photographs of everything from Walden's Pond to Plymouth Rock. They really study the various kinds of pines and shrubs peculiar to New England, and they gather shells on the beaches to put on the mantel at home. And I find, when I meet them, that my own horizon is widened as I hear about their home places and just what the weather is like in January. I am sure, incidentally, that there is no country in the world where weather is so interesting, since in our land we have all its varieties.

It is a sad commentary that the vast numbers of these visitors we enjoy so much are not counted, whereas the small number who are obnoxious are made the main topic of conversation. Unfortunately, it is bad news that makes headlines because it is more dramatic. We tend to count the juvenile delinquents rather than the normal youngsters who are certainly in greater number.

What we notice in midsummer tourist season is that all the roads are suddenly strewn with garbage tossed from departing cars and that kittens and puppies wander crying along the highways, dropped off en route. Raw holes appear where someone has dug up a treasure to take home. Roadside signs are torn up; lawn furniture left near the road vanishes. Mailboxes are knocked over.

Our first sad experience was when the wrought-iron Stillmeadow sign by the picket fence disappeared. It had come from a special place in Maine and had a really beautiful wrought-iron cocker in the middle of it. I've often wondered just where the thief could put it or whether it was finally thrown away.

I have done a lot of wondering about many things, but I have decided as far as summer tourists go that the explanation is simple. Wherever you go, you take yourself with you. You pack your suitcases, close the house, arrange with the neighbors to pick up the papers and the mail, cancel the milk delivery, and so on. Then you drive off down the road.

But you do not leave yourself behind. Wherever you travel, you are with yourself. Perhaps at home your behavior is irreproachable. You keep your lawn mowed, put out the garbage in covered containers, feed your cats and dogs, belong to church and civic organizations. But this may be because of the pressure of living where *everybody knows you,* and you go along with the standards of your town or city. Once you leave your home surroundings, you are unidentified, unless a traffic cop stops you and writes down your license number for a violation. So you can be exactly your self, and your basic personality emerges full blown. If you enjoy ruining a quiet country area, you do it because you will be gone so soon. If you think it is fun to steal anything from ashtrays to house signs, you do so. And if you don't want to bother with your cats and dogs, you can drop them off and forget them. If you shop, you can make off with extras at the markets, because you will not see the market people again.

There is no solution to this problem for those of us who live with a summer season. After Labor Day we can get the community to clean up the roadsides, take the trash to the dump, put up new road signs, fill in the holes, and so on. But we try to remember those who are the kind of people we naturally love, and we know their own communities must welcome them back. And there are many, many more of these, as we always decide every September.

"Met some nice people," says Jimmy de Lory as he fills my gas tank, "along with the stinkers who got a tankful and drove off without even paying. More nice ones than not, really!"

The problem of overcrowding in city living becomes more acute, and I read with interest all the ideas for solving it. Suburban living also has problems, which two of my young friends did solve. Dick worked in the metropolis and commuted from their house in the suburbs. Karen and the two small children stayed at home. Dick's story is typical:

"I left the house every morning practically at daybreak and drove to the station and took the local to the city. If the train didn't break down, I got to work on time and dashed madly to the station when I got through. If there was a club car, my commuter friends and I spent a couple of hours drinking martinis and by the time I got home I was bushed. Also it was night and the children were already fed and put to bed. Karen warmed up my supper, and we ate, and we were both too tired to do anything."

He shook his head and sighed, remembering. "On weekends I just managed to mow the lawn and do a few chores. I hardly knew my children. My job was just fine, but one day I figured out we didn't have much of a life, since on top of working full time I spent nearly four hours daily on the train. So we sat down and talked it all over—Karen was wonderful and never complained, but what were we doing with our lives? So I found a job in a small town, at not nearly as much money, and we packed up and moved. Now we are a family again, and we share a lot of living with ourselves."

I realize this wouldn't work for all young couples; it depends on a mutual attitude as to what is important. If the husband's only goal is to be president of the company, or if the wife dreams of $1,500 frocks as well as plenty of household help, it would be frustrating. One's sense of values must be the directive.

But I am very happy to know two who had the courage to choose what they really wanted and, as the fairy tale would say, "lived happily ever after."

❁   ❁   ❁

Full summer brings breathless days when sometimes the heat is so intense I feel I could dish it up with
a spoon, preferably to drop it on a cake of ice. Memory
is so short that we forget in January what August feels
like. Often during a heat wave, I try to imagine walking
in deep snow and seeing great icicles hanging from the
well house. Conversely, in January I think of my favorite chicory plants blooming along the old stone walls as
they now do. Chicory is a true sky-blue, and every plant
is its own bouquet.

The birds do not sing so much now, but the
cicadas make August's special music, and I love it. The
rich smell of corn pollen fills the air as the field corn
ripens. The whole smell of summer, in fact, is the
smell of ripeness, and I wish it could be distilled and
bottled. I even like the rather strong, musty fragrance
of goldenrod and am glad the experts have decided it
has nothing to do with hay fever.

We often have severe droughts in New England
this time of year, but the valiant petunias never give up,
and nothing makes such a gay garden as ruffled petunias
in white, rosy red, purple, pink. They do exude a thick,
sticky juice when you cut them, but a bunch of petunias
in a milk-glass container is delightful—and you can always wash your hands afterward. I have never been able
to keep chicory from a determined wilt as soon as I bring
it in, but this may be because I do not know whether to
dip the ends of the stems in boiling water, or whatever.
Thistles are now a rich purple, but I do not try to pick
them either.

There are two theories in my valley about defeating
the heat. One is to keep all windows shut all day, open

them at night, and shut them at sunrise. The other is to leave every window in the house open and let whatever breeze there may be drift lazily in. I prefer this, for I love open windows. And I feel stale air has a musty dampness to it. Years ago when I lived in a city apartment, the thing that bothered me most was the closed windows, for on the sixth floor of a very old building one didn't leave the windows up day and night. Especially with a Siamese cat, several cocker puppies, and a young daughter. Not to mention me! I do not like heights and, incidentally, may have established a record for taking visitors to the top of the Empire State Building and falling down on my knees and crawling back to the relative safety of the door.

But if you live at ground level, I think your windows are the most important part of your home. Whether your furnishings are Louis Quatorze or cast-offs, your windows overlook the matchless blue of the sky, the silver glow of a young moon, or the black-purple of piled storm clouds galloping. Looking out keeps you from fretting because the chores aren't done or the washing machine won't work or it is time to change the beds again (a chore I absolutely hate). The vast outside brings a sense of proportion to you and a kind of quietness.

As far as Amber is concerned, windows are for cats. She can sit on the narrowest sill, press her small self against the glass, and bask in the hottest sun, or in winter paw away at the falling snowflakes against the glass. Whenever she is not helping me type or wash dishes or make beds (and she loves this), she is on a window sill. If something interesting goes on outside, she switches her tail furiously. When a car comes to the gate, she hears it far down the road and flies to the kitchen window and then dashes to me to let me know. I call her my watch cat, because nobody could ever get in the yard without Amber announcing it, day or night. And she has a way of swiveling her head as she follows the progress of anyone coming in. If it happens to be one of her favorite people, such as the plumber, she parades to the door with her tail bolt upright. If it is a stranger, the tail gyrates wildly. For she is a very private cat, and I have never been able to talk her into putting out the welcome mat as a matter of diplomacy.

This was a surprise to me, since our cockers and Irish setters welcomed anybody and everybody, and whoever came in the door and sat down had a lapful of both at once. However, Art Baines, who handled Holly to her championship, told me not to underestimate Holly, for if anyone laid a hand on me, she would kill him.

In August I find I am suddenly tired of summer salads, cold mousses, iced soups, and all the rest of it. But the vegetables are at their best, and I do love vegetables. One of our favorite supper dishes is Baked Stuffed Cucumbers. Split large cucumbers lengthwise, remove the seeds, and steam the cucumbers, covered, in a little salted water until half-tender but *not* soft. Fill the center cavities with buttered bread crumbs, top with grated cheese, place in a baking pan, and pour over ½ inch liquid—half milk and half water (or chicken broth). Bake in a hot oven (400 degrees) for about 20 minutes. Serve on a hot platter deep enough so you can pour the milk stock over them. You may also stuff them with leftover meat or fish (creamed and with diced onion added). I find people who do not like cucumbers will take two helpings of this. If you do not use any stuffing but the crumbs and cheese, serve thin slices of cold sugar-cured ham or cold chicken with it and crusty wedges of garlic bread.

Another Stillmeadow favorite is August Cooler: Boil 4 cups water and 2 cups sugar together for five minutes. Add 2 cups fruit juice (pineapple, orange, grape, grapefruit, or cranberry). Unless you have used unsweetened grapefruit juice, add 4 tablespoons lemon juice. Freeze in a refrigerator tray. When partly frozen, remove and whip until smooth. Refreeze. Serve in tall, chilled glasses with ginger ale poured over it. Serves four to six.

Both of these recipes are a help when guests drop in at teatime and decide to stay until after supper.

As summer ebbs, there is a taste of fall in the air, but I have never been able to analyze it. The world is still full of ripeness, and noons are hot. The roadside stands blaze with color; pumpkins add their rich yellow to the vegetable gardens. Zinnias and marigolds splash patchwork hues. Wild roadside grasses feather out in cinnamons and mauves. Surely everything is the same.

But on one night as dusk deepens over the pond, I notice a cool mist is rising. And the twilight breeze is touched with chill. Do I imagine that the green of the maples is not so assertive? And is there a faint haze over the old apple orchard? And why do I suddenly look at the woodpile just to be sure it is as high as it should be?

The Full Sturgeon Moon rises over the swamp on a serene landscape. But slowly and as always nature follows her own pattern. And mankind cannot change it even in this superscientific era. We must still pick the blueberries now before it is too late. We must fill the house with gladiola, and we must clean the great fire-place and lay a good apple-wood fire.

And as I walk in the yard at moonrise to say my good night to the world, I find myself with a new mes-sage—may autumn bring us her own gifts as the leaves turn.

"Summer's lease hath all too short a date," as the gentle bard said long ago, and when I hear the cicadas on a dreamy August afternoon, I feel a sadness in my heart. Summer ebbs as the goldenrod spikes grow tawny and the last of the hay goes in from the upper meadow. Chicory blooms like blue stars along the roadsides, one of the loveliest of wild flowers. Heat simmers over the swamp, and the air breathes of pollen.

The grandchildren spend half the day in and around the pond and come in dripping. The brook is quieter as it runs down the wooded hill, and bird songs seem subdued. It should be a lazy dreaming time for us, too, but it is not. The string beans are at it again, as Jill always said, and there is corn to freeze; in fact, the whole garden demands work. One neighbor puts up dozens of jars of tomatoes, and I may say I do not think any canned tomatoes can compare, not even the most expensive whole ones.

Sweet cucumber pickles and cucumber and oil pickles have been favorites of mine since Mama used to make them, and there are all the relishes and the chut-ney—and Jean's green tomato relish, which is elegant. We used to put up summer squash, too. There is really no limit to what can go on in a country kitchen, storing the richness of summer against the long bitter winter ahead.

I think that we respond to the rhythm of nature more than we know. There must be kinship with the squirrels, who labor so diligently to store their nuts. I notice people who do not have gardens are restless, feeling subconsciously they must do something at this season. As I drive to the village, I see blankets blowing on the lines, rugs airing, men cutting kindling in back yards. And I remember how in nesting time women buy new curtains, have rooms painted, polish the furniture—in short, make their own nests while the birds dash about carrying grasses and feathers. (When we had a good many cockers, the nests were lined with cocker fur.)

Around the foundations of the very old houses, the owners now begin to pack brush or sacks of leaves to help keep out the cold. Stillmeadow has stone terraces around it which help, but the floors are never exactly tropical in January.

The wild blackberries ripen, and the grandchildren fill small baskets with them. They are spicy and tart and seedier than store-bought ones, but they are a treasure to the girls. Elderberries open purple clusters, too, and surely elderberry is the queen of jellies. I used to make wild-grape jelly, too, but gave it up after one disastrous day when I had hung the jelly bag to drip in the back kitchen, and the twine broke, and we had a sea of purple all over the room.

Of all the gifts late summer brings, my favorite is new potatoes dug before any sane person would dig them. They are smaller than pullets' eggs and look like pearls. Dropped in boiling salted and buttered water and cooked briefly, they should be served in chowder bowls for the main supper dish with extra butter, seasoned salt, and pepper added. Thin slices of sugar-cured country ham may be served too, but I settle for potatoes. They do not remotely resemble potatoes fully grown. Sometimes I like a little warm top milk in the bottom of the bowl too. At such a meal, I mislay the calories.

However, I am happy to say a good many experts now feel even dieters should eat some potatoes, because they have something no other vegetable has. And they also do something to raise the spirits in a special way.

In these days the fruits and vegetables we buy at the market have been brought in as fresh and as fast as possible. We take it for granted that we may have strawberries in January and oranges any old time, as well as lettuce and asparagus (although this gets pretty woody out of season). But freshly gathered vegetables and fruits have flavor and texture and richness—remember what I said about corn earlier?

And perhaps if you have labored to produce them, your sense of achievement adds an extra quality. I notice some of my friends decide every year never to have another vegetable patch. I hear about this most of the winter, and then I go to their houses for supper and find the seed catalogues all over the living room. Just one more time . . .

I do not want to imply that there is anything wrong with our markets, for I think we tend to take all our advantages in homemaking for granted. I love the village market and sometimes get dizzy when I see the vast amount of supplies from all over the world that we can

load in our carts whenever we wish. George and Joe
Tomey, who manage to have anything we want, are two
of my most admired friends. Because of them, our market is still a personal place where we gather for a visit,
discuss town affairs, hear about the newest baby, and feel
we are still a community despite the new throughways
and industrial plants gobbling up our farmlands.

I remember when George started a small shop, and
now it is really a super supermarket, and I admit most
supermarkets frighten me. But in the final analysis it is
people who make places, and George and Joe and his
charming wife, Peggy, can make any shopper feel at
home and *special*, not just an anonymous figure laying
out cash at the check-out counter.

When I walk through the market, I wonder how
many other shoppers stop to appreciate the benefits we
have in this age—so much is wrong with it, it is good to
find something to be thankful for. I see the shelves
stocked, and remember there was no sugar until the
thirteenth century, no buttered bread until the sixteenth, no soap until the seventeenth. Matches came in
around the nineteenth century, and until this century
there were no frozen foods.

Tea was so special it had a good deal to do with the
Revolution, and now I walk by shelves of tea—boxes of
tea bags, canisters of Constant Comment whole tea, English and Irish teas, powdered iced-tea mixes, more than
I can count. The frozen-food area hums gently as the
electricity purrs—and there was no electricity until the
nineteenth century.

I think, when we find so much to complain about,
we should spend a little time adding up what we have

and being grateful. I myself never open a box of tissues without being thankful I am not boiling up squares of linen.

Coming down Jeremy Swamp Road past the meadow and the swamp, I find my heart beats happily when I see the ancient farmhouse tucked in the midst of the giant sugar maples. I may have been gone two hours or I may have been on Cape Cod, but there is that re-cognition (not recognition), which is a joy. I think of a few devoted readers who have come to see Stillmeadow and write back they were shocked to see it right on the road and not set back, like Southern mansions or far-Western establishments.

But in 1690 men built their houses right by the road, or where they planned to dig out a road to make it easier in the deep winters. Barns were near the houses. Even in summer it was better to drive the wagons near the back door to carry in the firewood for the huge fire-places. Occasionally in our valley folk have moved the ancient house and set it way back in the woods or on a hill, but I know those houses are not comfortable, since they were not built to be anywhere but right by the road.

Many of us have nightmares about the day when our dead-end roads will be throughways; meanwhile, we are happy as we are. And I am sure I could never consent to having Stillmeadow uprooted and moved to a different spot, for the hand-dug cellar was meant for this house, and the well by the back door was dug there to be handy for the buckets to be dropped down on the long ropes and later wound down by a chain. The man who built my house chose wisely, for there was the pond below the house, fed by two brooks racing down the hill.

Down the long, inevitable march of time the pond silted in and now has to be excavated sometimes, but it is the same pond. On the hand-hewn stone foundation of an early cabin, we put our summer house without moving a stone. Legend has it that Indians camped by our pond before the white man took over, and we still find an occasional quartz arrowhead, and Jill often turned up pottery shards when she cultivated the vegetable garden which lay between the house and the pond.

I happen to like being rooted in the past, and as I get out of the car and open the gate in the picket fence, I stop to see how the shadows fall on the old hand-cut clapboards and the way the maples touch the sky above the steep roof. The lilacs reach to the eaves, and the wisteria is a jungle on the well house. The house was built around the central chimney, and the fireplaces still provide heat. In the past the cooking was done on the great fireplace in the keeping room. The old iron cranes are still there, and often in winter the iron soup kettle hangs over the fire, sending out savory smells as the soup bubbles. The borning room across the stair well from the keeping room has no fireplace, so I often imagine when a baby arrived in winter, the family carried stoneware jugs filled with hot water to tuck in the bed with mother and child, and heated blankets to wrap around them.

The coffin door at the foot of the ladder-steep stairs opens directly onto the flagstone path by the well house. This door always interests visitors from other parts of the country. It had a practical purpose, for it was possible to carry the coffins downstairs and out to the waiting wagons. We found it also made it easy for us to move old chests and pine four-posters to the upper floor. But in the early days it was bolted shut except in times of death.

We were told that a minister lived at Stillmeadow before the church was in use and held his Sunday services in what is now my downstairs bedroom. A small reed organ stood where my four-poster stands. Sometimes I can hear the faint silvery tones of the organ, and a sense of peace comes with them. When the minister died, the men of the congregation carried his coffin down the stairs and out of the coffin door but, instead of laying it in the wagon, they carried it by hand all the way to the cemetery some miles away, for he was greatly beloved by his parishioners.

Southbury's first church was built in 1732, so there was a pulpit for the minister from which he preached the stern sermons of the day and where the strains of "Old Hundred" rose to the roof. It is simple and beautiful with its slender spire rising into the sky. But I like to think of those services held in my room.

I believe a very old house holds its memories of all the lives that have been spent there. Some of them must have been sorrowful and some happy, some difficult, some easy. But there is an overtone of happiness in this house which most people feel as they come in.

"There's something about this house," they often say. "It gives me a good feeling. . . ."

Sometimes as they sit down by the hearth, they reach down and gently touch the floor with its wide hand-cut black-oak boards and hand-made square-headed nails. (I wonder why round-headed nails came in and when?) There are cracks between the boards in some places, and we were told by a carpenter that they could be fixed with new wooden inserts, but we rejected so much change. We only went so far as to put in a few screws near the kitchen door where the floor creaked. Long years of waxing have kept these floors shining so they seem to glow. And just walking on them gives most of us a sense of security difficult to explain.

Houses all have personalities, at least to me, quite apart from the furnishings and décor and style, but this sturdy, ancient farmhouse has a special gentleness built into it. It is one reason we never felt restless. I said traveling is all very well if you can get home at night. I would be willing to go around the world if I came back in time to light the candles and set the table for supper.

I do travel in my own way by picking up a book. I have visited Athens and climbed the Spanish Steps in Rome, which I once did before we had Stillmeadow. In five minutes I can be in the Caribbean or climbing the Alps. And I do go to Cape Cod to the house by the sea when the children come to keep the lights at Stillmeadow glowing. But this is a minor pilgrimage.

The ancient house speaks. A very old house talks a lot. I hear soft footsteps of long-gone owners, doors creak, floorboards sigh and, if there is a breeze, windows rattle. I do not think I would be happy in a soundless apartment.

The ancient houses are vanishing, every one with its story. When I drive to Woodbury by the same road along which Rochambeau and his troops marched, I see the elegant mansion where the French were entertained and the owner locked his wife in an upstairs closet because she was so beautiful. I wonder if she could hear the music of the ball and whether she then hated her husband or was secretly grateful that he felt her beauty would devastate the gallant French officers. After all, he must have appreciated that beauty more than many husbands would have.

Another favorite house on the road is the old Stiles farmhouse where the best maple syrup has been made for generations, and there is the house with slave quarters in the rear, and the house where runaway slaves were housed on their way to Canada. I like to think there was an Underground station just a few miles from Stillmeadow.

We cannot all live in houses filled with the past, but I am glad some of us cherish them. My very dear friends Jean and Oscar, for instance, have a gravestone in their cellar where a child was buried long, long ago. They would never redo that cellar, they say, because the gravestone belongs there.

As far as a new house is concerned, I feel we are responsible for what it is like, and this has nothing to do with whether it is a mansion or a cottage or a development dwelling resembling one pea in a peapod. I have been called a sentimentalist, and I do not argue, although there is a world of difference between sentiment and sentimentality, for one is real feeling and the other is superficial. In any case, I think any house absorbs the life lived in it and keeps it. And I always hope that, when families move into a house, they will decide to give it pleasant memories.

When I go into a house, I feel instantly whether it is happy or sad. One of my favorites is a small, very simple house. Whenever I step in the front door, I feel warmth and ease of heart. Another very exquisite house I visit makes me feel a sadness.

Pursuing this thought as I dish up Amber's supper, I realize we are a part of our surroundings in a way that has nothing to do with our economic status or our locale. And we impress our personality on everything we come in contact with, which gives us an extra responsibility.

In the long run, we are our own destiny.

When Jill and I built the spanking new cottage on Cape Cod to spend some time listening to the thunder of the surf at Nauset and the lonely cry of seagulls on Mill Pond, I felt ill at ease. Everything crackled with newness. It took me some time to get used to sleeping in a regular bed instead of my own at home with the pine-apple-tipped posts and the holes in the frame where the ropes used to go in the days when it was a rope bed— maybe with a featherbed on top. I was homesick for the great fireplace and for my old iron Dutch oven. And I worried about the barn cats and the birds, even though the children were at Stillmeadow, taking care of everything handsomely and having a chance, as the saying goes, to lead their own lives without being interfered with.

But one thing I said, "We must store up good memories here, and we must be careful about it." And even now if someone who drops in begins a tirade about something, I am patient for a very short time and then say mildly, "Let's not talk about this any more."

I am sure Stillmeadow, since 1690, has shared in everything that can possibly happen to human beings, but the loving care of the first builder left a heritage which in a small way I hope the Cape house may also leave.

The ending of summer brings a feeling of change in the rhythm of life. And soon the school bus will roar down the road. From the big houses and the small, children pour out and with them comes the hope of tomorrow, but I always hope the house they come back to is not an unhappy one, for making a safe, secure home place for them is what parents must do.

Being good parents is, in my opinion, a rewarding if difficult career. Women who are bored with homemaking and being a wife and mother should take a long look at themselves. Being bored comes from within themselves. Boredom is, in fact, easily cultivated if you work at it, and it is a kind of blindness.

There is enough drama in any family to provide a challenge, and whatever intelligence a woman has gets full exercise. As for rewards, they cannot be counted. Nobody in any so-called career is indispensable, but when a wife and mother so much as goes off for a change and rest, a replacement is impossible. And I believe it is basic in the feminine temperament to long to be important, to be needed. I think we are more personal than most men, because nature has made us that way.

I have read a lot of articles of late by experts who feel the family is a doomed institution and a kind of communal living is better. But I think we would have a strangely disordered world if we gave up the family as a unit. And I hope this theory will be abandoned before we become a rootless, disorganized people.

I think of a simple illustration. We spent a good

many years raising cockers and Irish setters and belonged to what we called the dog world. We traveled as far as Canada to meet and enjoy dog people. From long experience I may state that puppies raised impersonally in the best and most elegant kennels never quite measured up to those raised personally, who came in and out of houses, were talked to, played with, and loved as individuals. I feel that children also develop faster and with fewer personal difficulties if they are raised in a family group and not institutionalized.

When I investigated, I discovered the champions invariably had handlers or owners who made them a focal point of life. In short, the great champions had personal, individual devotion and care, and this was partly why they became champions, not just because their configuration was superb.

Sometimes, when I have spent too much time thinking about problems, I decide to rest my spirit. I read Keats's poetry or reread some of *Hamlet* or, if I am in a different mood, I read Beverley Nichols. I finish with anything of Hal Borland's, for he widens my horizons immediately. Some of my favorite books are springing apart at the seams, and I try to shore them up with Scotch tape. (I wonder why it is called Scotch?)

My father gave me a set of Shakespeare, all the volumes bound in maroon leather and embossed with gold. I have never sent it to be rebound, because I cherish it too much to entrust it to the current postal system. So when I pick up a volume, I have to hold it together with both hands. My Keats fared better, for I have so many copies—one in every room. My books are my friends, and

I feel sad about people who miss the excitement and satisfaction of having books in their lives.

"I never have any time to read," says one of my close friends.

This is nonsense. For instance, you can take a book with you when you go to the dentist, the doctor, or a meeting. You always have to wait, and you can read while you wait. If you even go to the filling station and wait for the tires to be checked and the tank filled and the oil put in, you can pick up the book on the seat beside you and *read*. You can also read while you wait for the washing machine to go into the rinse cycle, when you are scheduled to add the softener. You can read while you wait for the plumber or electrician—and these can be long waits—or while you are under the dryer at the beauty parlor.

I have never known anybody, male or female, who doesn't spend a lot of time just waiting. But if you have the habit of tucking a book in your bag, you will reap a rich reward from the waiting hours. The one thing I advise against is carrying an Agatha Christie mystery, because you may have to stop just when the murderer is about to be found.

Serious nonfiction or poetry is my choice, for you can read a paragraph or a verse and then let it blossom in your mind while the filling-station man, for instance, decides you have a valve leak in the right front tire.

Now the Full Sturgeon Moon is rising over Jeremy Swamp, and I put down the book I am deep in and go out to visit with the moonlight. As summer ends, I can feel the change in the air although I cannot describe it. There is a sense of nature herself becoming still as the richness of growth ends. It is a green world, and the night air is balmy, and tomorrow will be fair. But the mysterious forces are at work in leaf and stem and stalk. Autumn writes her signature in the zinnias.

AUTUMN

B̲y our man-made calendar, Labor Day is summer's end. The rhythm of our life changes, for school is beginning. Vacations are over and also the last desperate getting together of clothes for school. In our family it always turns out that Alice and Anne have absolutely *nothing to wear!*

Sometimes we are all on Cape Cod during this time, and I go to Watson's with the girls and their mother. I feel that the new generation knows more about clothes than I did when I went to college. At thirteen and eleven, Alice and Anne know exactly what they want and whether the neckline is right and the sleeves the kind they prefer. Clothes for the young are charming and light years away from the middy blouses and pleated navy skirts I remember. There are endless combinations in two-piece costumes and color ranges from tangerine to firehouse red to emerald to lemon-and-lime mixes.

By the time we get to the shoes, I am dizzy and just sit quietly in the shoe department while the boxes pile up. By then I am hungry, for shopping always has that effect on me. Eventually we do get out and go to the

Lobster Claw for lunch, where the girls eat enough to sustain a rescue squad and Connie and I count the calories.

It all bears out my theory that children are more advanced in every way than when I was a child. In those days Mama and Papa decided what I was to wear, and I wore it. Now Alice and Anne make their own decisions and know what they will wear and what they will not. Let anybody try to persuade them to don a single costume they do not feel is right—there is another lost cause.

Later on when the children are all set and have finished all the lobster in sight, we go home to show the wardrobes to Daddy, who has spent a quiet day working on some manuscript or fishing with a neighbor. His role is to approve and admire the fashion show. After which the girls get back into ragged pants and faded jerseys and take off for the beach to gather treasures. When they fly in with tangled hair, smelling of dead fish, they have lost their sophistication.

I myself am a poor shopper and try never to shop for my own clothes without my beloved friend Millie. Millie could have been a designer and couturière, among her other talents, and her patience is inexhaustible. My tendency to take the first dress I see in my size horrifies her. She belongs to the school that believes in *trying it on!* So she and the nice saleslady select what they think might look fairly presentable, and I try things on, smothering in one of those cubicles in the store.

As long as anything is blue or lilac, I am satisfied. But Millie and the sales girl stand off and inspect me with pursed lips (and this is the only time anyone does view me with pursed lips).

"Well, it doesn't *do* anything for her," comments Millie.

"I think perhaps the shoulders . . ."

"The neck is wrong," says Millie firmly, "and it is too long in the waist."

This continues until something turns up that not only fits well but *does* something for me.

At times they each take a pinch of the garment under inspection to see if alteration would be possible, and they always decide that that wouldn't help enough.

By the time Millie and I have finished a day's shopping, I have everything I need for the season except self-confidence. Often we go out to dinner that night with her husband, and if he looks at me and says, "Well, you look good tonight," I know Millie's struggles have been worth it. If he doesn't notice I am not wearing the same navy slacks and familiar light-blue top, I feel discouraged.

And then Millie comments, "Now you have all you need for a while, but I suppose you'll wear the same old things day and night and just leave the new ones hanging in the closet!" And, as usual, she is right, for I feel more comfortable in old clothes than in new.

I have one or two friends who love to shop just as recreation. Whenever they have a free afternoon, they go shopping, not with any idea of buying anything, just to browse around the racks the way I would browse through book stacks. The harried sales girls do their best but never ring up a single sale. But my friends make no pretense—they say they are "just looking."

At the other extreme is the kind of woman such as Millie and I saw at Edson's one day. The store was jammed with buyers, but this woman had tried on and rejected a huge pile of dresses before we came in, and she went on trying on every single dress in her size, along with some that weren't. She was waited on by one of my favorite saleswomen, Mrs. Ray, and as Mrs. Ray went by with another armful, I whispered to her, "Why don't you tell her to go home?"

Eventually the woman left without buying anything and without a word of thanks.

"There are always some like that," said Mrs. Ray patiently.

Most saleswomen are kind and helpful, I notice, even when the shoppers are impatient or rude. I think a great deal can be discovered about a woman's personality by her manner in the store. And this reminds me of a remark Millie and I overheard at lunch one day.

"It took me years," said the woman at the next table, "to teach Charlie that a waitress was *not* a lady."

I was tempted to say, "Neither are you a lady!"

One of my favorite shops is Beth Bishop's on the Cape, and I have watched the staff there during tourist season, when a good many women come in to look because it's not a good beach day. They are always welcomed with gentle courtesy, and if they do buy a scarf or so, they are thanked as much as if they had bought a two-hundred-dollar suit.

I suppose what my observation leads to is that whatever our walk of life may be, we bring ourselves to it subconsciously. I do know of one salesclerk who is so unpleasant that, when I go into that particular store and see her, I turn around and creep out. Another one in that same place makes me feel I am a real friend. These two are presumably paid the same wage and work under exactly the same conditions, but they are worlds apart in temperament and adaptability. One obviously resents the world and everyone in it, and the other finds pleasure in helping distracted shoppers find what they want.

There is a so-called department store I visit which has everything but organization. Merchandise is piled at random all over, and one threads a way through labyrinthian aisles. In this store there are several salesclerks who deserve medals.

"Well, I don't see any more shower curtains like that here," says one. "I'll just run down cellar and see if I can't find what you want."

"We should have more pillows in the attic," says another, "I'll run up and see." They always add, "It's no trouble at all!"

And miraculously they find what they are hunting for, although I cannot imagine what the cellar and attic look like as far as organization goes. And they enjoy the triumph of finding the treasures almost as much as if they were their own.

In the big cities one seldom knows any of the staff in the huge stores, but in Southbury and on the Cape living is not so impersonal. And I feel we suffer from the impersonality of our age and need to realize we are all kin.

Habit is a strange power. Now I fall into the habit of watching the school bus go down Jeremy Swamp Road, even though I have no small persons boarding her. I acquired this particular habit when Erwin, the neighbor boy, came into my life. He was about ten at that time, and he came over every day after school. If the bus was late, I began to stand at the window and wait for it. It stopped at the corner by the mailboxes, and when snow was falling, it had a hazy look as it ground to a stop.

Then a small, wrapped-up figure would toil down our road, and the world was secure again. Now Erwin is away at school, but I still watch for that bus and imagine the thin, earnest figure coming home. I miss making the hot cocoa and popping in a soft marshmallow to melt on the top of the mug. I miss the conversations we had, although Erwin could never be called an easy talker. Usually all he ever said about school was that it wasn't too bad.

He was so good in mathematics that he took over all my adding and subtracting and dividing, although he could hardly spell "cat." But we began to play word games, and we put up a paper on the kitchen bulletin board and added words every day which he had learned to spell. That list would have horrified any regular teacher, because it consisted of words chosen at random from conversation and included "minestrone" from the grocery list and "ecology" and "effete" and "sonnet" and "antibiotic." When the chores were done, we played Scrabble and usually ended in gales of laughter. And then Erwin would tell me how simple long division is.

Now when I see a school bus swinging down Jeremy Swamp Road, I think of the youngsters going home. They are the future of America, and I hope it will be a better world for them, with no wars to end wars and with opportunities to live in security.

We hear so much about what is wrong with education that sometimes I wonder what is right. I sit in on a lot of discussions about whether grading should be abolished, no required subjects expected, no fixed class hours set up. It is, I reflect, a long march from that one-room schoolhouse which still stands in the village and is used as a museum.

And it is a long march, too, since the days I carried my report card timidly to Papa. If I failed to get A in everything, the house exploded, and Mama had to dry my tears. Unfortunately, I usually got C in mathematics and early developed an inferiority complex that has been with me ever since.

I once got an A for the simple reason that I had a crush on the teacher. And this teacher happened to be one of those rare, gifted ones. The rest of my time, even through college, I was always punished one way or another for those miserable C's. The gulf between B and C was never out of my mind. Had there been no grading, my life would have been much happier.

As for required subjects—they all were. It took a special dispensation for me to have one or two *extra* courses in English literature in college, but I had to take more math, as well as French, botany, geology, Bible, art, and so on.

Fixed class hours were firm as a concrete wall, and the only way to avoid one was to have a temperature of 102—and the doctor's note.

Education was not exactly free and easy; except for an occasional trip to the Boston Art Museum or a field trip for geology, it was conducted in the classroom. I am therefore amazed at the way students wander around these days and get credit for it.

When I was a beginning writer, I wasted a lot of time bewailing the fact that I had not been able to take writing courses and literature to my heart's content.

But now I wonder. On thinking it all over, I believe

some type of grading is important, not just an S for satisfactory. If I received a B in Shakespeare, I knew I had not worked as hard as I should, and I tried harder. I knew where I stood, and it mattered. After one C— in math I sat up half the nights trying to make sense out of what seemed impossible. It showed in the next C+. I now realize the difference between a minus and a plus is rather slim, but it wasn't then.

On the other hand, grading brings on a special kind of snobbery. Students who get straight A's in everything tend to acquire the habits of royalty, which can be very trying. Also many things affect grading, particularly the ability of the teachers. And often the straight A's are fortunate in the classes they are assigned to. They are likely to get the best teachers, and usually the best class hours. Early morning hours are fine for morning people but deadly for those like me who are at their best after being fortified with lunch.

Finally, no two teachers really grade alike, for personality is involved. I have known two teachers to grade duplicate examination papers with a difference of enormous span. Some teachers feel the lowest grade possible is more of a stimulus, whereas others feel the highest encourages the student.

As for required subjects, I have come to believe they are a good idea. They widen the horizon. We live in a complex world of infinite variety, and the more we know of all subjects the better off we are. I happened to love German, but I had four years of it in high school, so I was forced to take French in college. Four more years of German would have been most valuable and so would more Latin. However, the required French, miserable as it made me, gave me a smattering of French—at least enough to translate menus in an elegant French restaurant and understand a few phrases in some book I am reading.

My own teaching experience was confined to writing courses, elective and not required, and grading wasn't much of a problem, because it is all too easy to evaluate a manuscript. Being elective meant the students wanted to take these courses, and although the hours were supposed to be fixed, they often ran over until it was time to close up the classroom.

My suggestions for changes in education begin with the elementary schools. This covers an age group when learning a language is easiest, and I believe languages should be taught in very early grades, beginning with Latin. Our curious language is chiefly based on Latin, and with an understanding of Latin it is not hard to define almost any unfamiliar word by knowing the root.

And since the world is growing smaller, and we are not going to be an isolated country any longer, I believe at least two other languages should be part of the curriculum. I have been told that in the United States fewer people speak a foreign language than in any other country in the world. We need to communicate with those in other countries, and language is communication.

Secondly, I believe we should teach history to all students, for a study of history gives us an understanding of what moves mankind and what direction we should take as we make new history.

And perhaps most of all we need to teach English. There is no substitute for words, and our own tongue is our basic tool. I listen to various youngsters and men and women being interviewed on television, for example. Ninety percent cannot speak our own language with

any ease. After a question, the typical response consists of "A . . . a . . . ah . . . ah . . ." Or, "Well . . . well
. . . a . . ." The grammar is atrocious. They are confused, quite naturally, because they can find no words
to express what they want to express. This is not confined to our super-athletes and astronauts. I brace myself
and wait for the "ahs" and "wells." Sometimes it goes
"Well, ah, it's like . . . ah . . . I mean it is like . . ."

I believe by the time a boy or girl graduates from
high school, or in fact, from eighth grade, he or she
should be able to utter a few sentences of good solid
English. Sometimes on television everything is written
out, and this may also be painful, because reading seems
too difficult.

I have grown more or less accustomed to the tire-
some use of "like" for "as," but I wonder about degrad-
ing the English language as much as we do. My bête noire
comes in government speeches. "We shall continue on,"
is the phrase. "Continue" means to "go on" so "continue
on" might as well be changed to "go—go—go!"

Obviously it is not lack of intelligence that makes it
so difficult for people to put together a decent sentence.
This must rest squarely on the shoulders of our educa-
tional institutions, and something should be done about
it immediately.

So as I watch the school bus with its precious
freight, I hope the educators will change a few of their
ideas about what is essential.

The turning year brings a change in the valley, as
the first leaves begin to turn to gold and scarlet. It is no
longer the green, green world of summer. Suddenly one

morning I look out and see the swamp maple ablaze. I feel the strangeness of nature all over again. For every growing tree and plant goes by some inner clock, no two ever alike. Why don't they all change color at the same time? The giant sugar maples around Stillmeadow are presumably the same age, planted by that farmer so many years ago. Their roots go down into the same soil, the same winds and suns affect them, the rains fall without favor on all of them. The temperature is exactly the same.

But there is one outside my bedroom window that always has the rich dark sap running down the huge trunk *first* in February and March. It has the first cloud of green to canopy the house. And now it is the first to be tinged with gold in autumn. And when the leaves fall like quiet rain, this one will have leaves at her feet before the rest. Those on either side stay green longer. If anyone could explain this, it would be Hal Borland, who knows more about the ways of nature than anyone I have ever been privileged to know. But he has not written about this mystery.

The swamp maple is easier to explain, for it stands with feet in water, and the swamp water must change from the still heat of summer to a cooling temperature. Now that the scientists have discovered plants have emotions, I wonder whether this tree isn't emotionally more ready for the killing frost. Perhaps it is like some women who try to live ahead. Perhaps it is so sensitive that the first cool autumn night makes it decide to go on and get it all over with. I shall, of course, never know. But when this tree begins to turn, I know autumn has come, and it is time to say farewell to the richness of summer. And time to get ready for the autumn rains and the first frost and to think about taking in some of the lawn furniture.

The Full Harvest Moon is the color of a ripe peach and brings a mellow glow to a quiet earth. Some leftover katydids still echo the song of summer, but the night air feels as if it had been dipped in the cool running brook.

I have always known it would happen someday. I am scared of electrical appliances, and I have never been one who could give a refrigerator a good firm kick and have it start going again. Vacuum-cleaner hoses have a way of clogging as soon as I plug them in. The fluorescent lights in the bathroom burn out, and I study the directions as I try to figure out how to get a new tube in. The light goes on for five minutes, and I am intoxicated by my brilliance. Then the light goes out. It seems that the tube is defective.

I have trouble with the top units of my range, because if I take them out to clean, they never sink back into position as they should. They slant. Also the preheat on the oven keeps preheating long after I have theoretically turned it off and am on 325 degree bake for lamb roast.

But disaster really struck when I turned on the disposal this morning, and the resulting sound was like a bomb going off. The whole kitchen shook. I turned off the motor and gingerly inserted one helpless hand in those dark, dank innards. What I found was one of my best teaspoons, hopelessly mangled. It was bent double, and the bowl looked as if a tractor had run over it.

Obviously that teaspoon had somehow washed into

the drain, although I shall never know how it managed to do it. Then I had the problem of whether to run the disposal again with a stream of cold water or just leave it alone for a week or so to rest up. Finally I had some coffee and pulled myself together. I turned it on, and it ran normally. I decided not to worry about the state of the blades that had tried so hard to eat up a thick stainless-steel spoon, but I promised I would put only lettuce leaves in for a while.

I have a friend who can use her disposal for chop bones, chicken bones, melon rinds, and all kinds of things, but mine will not eat up one teaspoon.

I get along pretty well with my pop-up toaster, as long as I do not try to change the setting. Sometimes the toast pops up crisp as a cinder; at other times it comes out pale enough to suggest it needs vitamins. Whether I push the button to "light" or "dark" makes no difference; it has a mind of its own. Fortunately I like toast any way, with the exception of toast in the English manner, which means it is put in silver racks so it cannot stay hot a single minute. (I have one of the elegant English silver toast racks, which I use as a file for unanswered mail.)

We have wells both at Stillmeadow and on the Cape, and the water is pumped up by earnest little motors. I have learned that when a well motor runs all night, whether you even draw one glass of water or not, the proper procedure is to push an emergency "off" button and call the plumber-electrician in the morning. This same treatment also goes for the furnace motor. A sensible furnace goes off now and then, especially when the temperature gets above 85 degrees. If I wake up at midnight and have been dreaming I am in the sub-sub tropics, I push another red button.

As for kitchen utensils, I am very cozy with my pressure cooker, since the one time I forgot to put the jiggle top on and had beautiful boiling-hot chicken soup all over the ceiling. But when time permits, I use the old cast-iron Dutch oven, which I have had for over thirty years. One friend says it shows I belong in an earlier age, and another—my scientific friend Helen— spent a good deal of time trying to explain all about electricity and gave up when I admitted I could not understand just how it got into things.

A year or so ago I bought a range with a self-cleaning oven. The reason was that it made me dizzy to stand on my head and try to clean the back part of the oven. The range was installed at the Cape by two very nice men, who managed to chop up pieces of the old one, take off three doors, and get it out to the yard. Then I waited until Millie, my mainstay, came to clean house, and we decided we might turn on the oven cleaner.

We both had some coffee and read the instruction book. The new range bristled with buttons and little red lights, but we found something labeled "self-clean" and pushed a button. It was about eleven thirty, and I started lunch (which was to be Welsh rarebit). Suddenly the kitchen began to smell like a glue factory. The air was dense. An hour later we were reading the instruction book again and having more coffee and getting hungrier by the minute.

"I don't think we better turn on anything else," said Millie.

"No, let's just turn this off."

But the oven had no idea of being turned off; it was minding its own business. So we opened all the windows and called Snow's and fortunately located the range man. We both talked over the phone, confusing him considerably, but after ten minutes he said firmly, "It will go off when it's ready. You have a temperature of over fourteen hundred degrees, and it takes half an hour to cool down. Meanwhile, you cannot open the oven door."

"We found that out," I said.

"And how soon may I use one top burner?" I asked.

"Oh, the top burners have nothing to do with it," he assured me.

"It didn't say anything about this taking three hours," I said.

"No, I'm sorry, but the new instruction sheet didn't happen to explain that," he said. "But just *don't worry*. Call me back if it doesn't go off in another half hour."

Somewhat shaken, we finally sat down to our Welsh rarebit. Much later the smell from the oven diminished, and we were able to breathe as if we had recovered from an asthma attack.

The nice man called back, and I think was reassured to find us both very vocal.

"But when we self-clean that oven," I said, "we'll do it in the middle of the afternoon and stay out of the kitchen."

I am happy to report that the next time we experimented the smell was less, and the oven was undeniably sparkling when we finally dared to open the door (and it was willing to open). However, I notice Millie has a habit of wiping up the inside of the oven by hand unless a casserole has laid a patina of cream sauce all over it. The one thing we really learned from the instruction book was to take out all the racks or they would turn blue. I would never discourage anyone from a self-cleaning oven range, but I would point out that it has problems.

And when we got the new washing machine, I asked Mr. Snow to sell me the one with the fewest knobs and buttons. He sold me the simplest one they had. But he had to call up to say this model was no longer in stock so he would send the next and newer model—which he did. When I saw the battery of knobs, I asked the man who installed the machine to give it a trial run.

"It's perfectly simple," he said. "You can't go wrong."

He didn't know me very well. I read the instruction book three times, and I read the writing inside the cover of the machine. I read all the words by the knobs—"cold," "warm," "hot," "cold," "permanent press." Then I did a hand washing and waited for Millie. By now I can manage by leaving everything set exactly the same as she does.

The new refrigerator with the self-defrosting unit is, so far as I know, the one piece of equipment that a child could manage, and that is because you are not supposed to do anything about it. The installer set the temperature and nothing would persuade me to tinker with it. The freezer unit purrs away, and it really defrosts—and runs 80 percent of the time—but it is relatively quiet. When I get discouraged about any of the other pieces of equipment, I go out and admire my refrigerator.

I am a great fan of Ralph Nader's. And if I should ever meet him, I would ask him to start one of his crusades to simplify all household equipment. I do not even want an alarm clock in my radio. I tell the time by my old watch.

I do not mean I would like to go back to the days of oil lamps, water hauled from the well in a bucket, or unheated houses—or any of what we call the good old days. But I do think that the technological age can be overpowering and that a good many modern aids to living are unnecessarily complicated, especially since every complication adds a possibility of something's going wrong.

When we first came to Stillmeadow, we cooked on an ancient cast-iron stove. It had a reservoir on one side which kept hot water at hand. It was a wood stove and ate up good-sized chunks of wood at a remarkable rate. In winter we had to get up in the night to feed it, since it was also the only heat in that part of the house. The oven was always warm, and if the door were left open, a comforting deal of heat came from it. It was also fine for drying out mittens and jackets or warming dinner plates or keeping roast beef warm (not all of these at once, of course).

The heat on the top could be graduated by pushing pots farther back or nearer to the front, and it was possible to adjust that heat far better than the new push buttons can. The day the old stove finally had to be taken out, I stayed out of the house. But sometimes on a midwinter midnight I am glad I do not have to get up and open the woodshed door and haul out a big chunk of wood. It is pleasant to turn up the electric blanket and bask.

And then during a 30 below night, "the electric" may go off, and I feel the air in the house congealing around me and think wistfully that, if only that dear old range were there, I could put in some more wood, draw the old pine rocker up by the open oven door, and read a good book in warmth and comfort.

Electricity is definitely the lifeblood of the house nowadays. One tree limb falling on one cable down the road can plunge every house in darkness and cold, and even the great fireplace in the keeping room cannot heat the whole downstairs.

I often think the early residents of my 1690 house were a sturdier breed than we are today. In January they took soapstone slabs to bed, which had been heated by the open fire. Some people used hot bricks. The lovely four-posters they slept in were weighted down with patchwork quilts or down puffs and handmade blankets. They could wear long-sleeved woolens to bed and many men and women wore nightcaps as well and knitted bed socks. But there was always that moment when they had to get up at some ungodly hour to build up the fires in all the fireplaces (Stillmeadow had three downstairs and two upstairs). It took stamina to step out on the frigid floors, get dressed in chilly clothes, and *get breakfast* after stoking up the fire in the range.

It's no wonder they had pancakes, fried eggs, hot muffins, bacon or sugar-cured ham slices, and maybe a piece of apple pie with their coffee. The toast and juice and black coffee of today would have horrified any good homemaker.

I can see the old well house from the kitchen window. The great iron wheel that the bucket rope hung from is still there, and as I turn on the faucet for the coffee water, I wonder whether I would have been able to go *outdoors* in January and wind that wheel around to let the bucket down and wind it back up. As for doing a washing, I would have folded up before I drew enough water to fill one washtub.

Then, too, I enjoy a hot shower with plenty of water. I can't imagine filling one of those tin tubs by hand and then having to empty it. The tub used to be brought out on Saturday nights in the old days and set in front of the range, and the family, in turns, had their weekly baths. Then the tub was retired until the next week. Nobody had heard of bath oil or bath sprays, but the hand-made soap was ready in nice chunks. I have a friend who still makes it because she likes it.

So in spite of my problems with equipment, I admit I am grateful that life is, on the whole, easier. And perhaps most of all, much as I love candlelight, I would not like to read by it.

I also think that, in this superefficient civilization, there is a place for those of us who find we need help. I find I have great satisfaction when someone needs my own help in the few areas in which I have some skill, such as cooking. I am happy when a neighbor rushes over to consult me about a recipe or wants to know how to concoct a casserole that will serve twelve people or wonders what herbs are best for certain dishes or what wine goes with what.

And having raised cockers and Irish setters for years, I feel pleased to undertake almost any problem, such as whelping, feeding, training, and what to do if a cherished dog eats the linoleum or bites the mailman. I can spend a long time figuring out how to persuade a dog to heel free or do the sit-stay on command, and when my advice turns out to solve things, I am radiant.

Then I greatly enjoy having someone drop in with an assortment of wild-eyed flowers that must be arranged to go in the church the next day and now simply lie down all over the containers.

I also have helpful advice for young writers about manuscripts, having spent half a lifetime on mine. This usually boils down to a firm suggestion to throw away the first third and go on from there.

I am no gardener, but I am a fine African-violet expert. Friends are always bringing me ailing African violets, and sometimes go away looking back dubiously because I have suggested they did not talk to them enough, and there must be some conflicts in the house.

When I am feeling especially inferior because of a losing battle with an appliance, I comfort myself with the fact that I can refinish furniture to any queen's taste and know all about adding some white vinegar to the water when trying to get a stain from a blond rug.

Life is, after all, a matter of balance. Were we all equally gifted in all areas, it might be a very dull world. And there is no use in worrying about what we cannot do. If we use any ability and skill we have to the utmost, we can still be of use in this world, which has infinite needs in infinite areas.

Too often someone says to me in despair, "I cannot do this. . . . I cannot do that. . . ." I even hear this from some friend who can make a gorgeous hostess robe out of a couple of old bath towels. Or someone who can hardly fry an egg without turning it to solid rubber but can get out an extension ladder and climb to the roof and clean out clogged eaves. Or someone who is paralyzed at the thought of making an announcement at a club meeting but always says the right thing to anyone in trouble.

We all have dreams of what we might have been. But it is better to be happy with whatever gifts we do possess—and to use them to the fullest. Sometimes it is a good idea to make a list of what we can do and are good at doing instead of feeling resentful about our shortcomings.

It may be that happiness is as simple as accepting what we are and never envying those who seem to be endowed with other gifts.

I happen to be passionately fond of music and come from a long line of musical near-geniuses. I cannot carry a tune. At one time in my life I felt crushed, especially since my father said there was no use buying me a violin as I had no ear for music. Later I began to realize that music also has to be listened to, and I can listen better than a good many other people I have known. I seem to sink in a tide of the great music— Bach and Beethoven, for instance. I become part of it. I also love folk music, country and western, which is part of our national heritage. And I enjoy old-fashioned nostalgic music from an earlier era. I would find a great deal in rock music if it didn't hurt my ears. So I can listen to the great operas without feeling inferior because I cannot sing like Beverly Sills. I am just grateful I can listen.

My final thought about coping with the daily round of living is that the learning process is very important. For me, even learning finally to manage not to have "preheat" going on the range all the time I am baking a cheese soufflé is a triumph. It eases the inferiority feeling I have when I cannot make the stereo drop just one record at a time. Sometimes it does, but sometimes, with the same records on, four or five will drop with a thud. Of course, it only means I have to leave the typewriter more often to start it again, but it is frustrating. I remind myself that at least I can now manage the "preheat" and "bake" and "broil" with remarkable ease.

I read a great deal nowadays about the brain, which has always been mysterious. Presumably somewhere in it is stored all the knowledge we have ever acquired as well as the capability of acquiring more. Mine is a strange storehouse on which I can reflect, as I reread the book, on how to do permanent press in the washing machine. If I can quote, as I often do, many of Keats's sonnets, why can't I remember the instructions for the laundry?

I leave this for those experts who feel they can fool around with the brain and change the various patterns, even to changing personality.

On a chilly autumn day we like Leek and Potato Soup. It makes a fine supper by the fire. To make this soup, you need fresh leeks and white onions diced to make 3 cups, 3 tablespoons butter, 3 tablespoons flour, about 4 cups of hot water, 4 cups potatoes diced or cut

in chunks, 1 teaspoon seasoned salt, the green part of
the leeks, and milk to make the consistency you like.

Cook the leeks and onions in the butter for five
minutes (until golden but not brown). Add the flour
and cook 2 minutes, stirring until blended. Remove
from heat and add the hot water, then the potatoes, salt,
and green part of the leeks (you may not want to use
them all). Simmer for 30 to 40 minutes, then add milk
slowly to thicken the soup. Do not let it boil. Serves
four to six.

This is the basic leek soup. Serve in hot soup bowls
sprinkled with chopped parsley or chives. It is the most
versatile soup, for you may add three cubes of squash
with the potatoes or a few green beans or Brussel sprouts
or a few lettuce leaves. You may put it through a sieve
for a creamy soup or leave it as is if you like the potato
chunks in it.

My life with Blackberry began, as many important
relationships do, quite accidentally. I certainly never
expected to adopt a wild skunk. The children were
visiting me on Cape Cod, and Anne, the eleven-year-old
granddaughter, skimmed in one day at dusk in great
excitement.

"We have a happening! Gram, there are three
skunks by the birdbath."

One was very large and slightly tarnished, one was
plump and prosperous as a banker, one was small.

All of them were obviously hungry, nipping up bits
of bread left by the birds.

"I'd better take them a handout," said my son-in-
law. When he went out, they scuttled down the steep

bank that leads to the beach, but the minute the food was out, they sidled back and gobbled.

"They are getting ready to hibernate," said Curt. "They have to eat a lot."

The next afternoon we were sitting with cocktails on the lawn when three pointed noses poked through the wild roses by the split-rail fence. When a nice aluminum pie plate of food was served, they ambled to it. They ate minced roast beef, cat kibbles, bits of cheese, milk. They left one lettuce leaf. Then they took the tin with them.

We could see their den down the bank, for a big fall of dirt marked the entrance right in the middle of the brush and briar roses and poison ivy and scrub pines. In a few days it was also marked by five pie tins and two cat-food cans. So our first problem was how to keep the slope from looking too much like the town dump. The only way to collect the tins would be to creep on hands and knees through the poison ivy. The tins stayed.

"Oh, well, they will stop coming soon," said Curt.

By the time the children left for the city, we had found a heavy cake tin for a feeding dish, a square, double-thick one, not easy to lug. Any cat-food tin was carried off by the small one, now named Blackberry.

A good many casual visitors who drove up and saw five of us sitting in the yard with three skunks ambling around usually stayed in their cars. Regular guests were directed to the door at the other end of the house and came in through the wing. Occasionally someone said, "If they come in my yard, I'll shoot them."

Meanwhile, I kept on learning about them. They

drank from rain puddles, so I got out the heavy ceramic water dish that belonged to my beloved Irish setter and kept fresh water in it. They drank water extravagantly, leaning their forepaws on the bowl and dipping their noses in. They drank before dinner, during dinner, after dinner.

By late fall, when the cold east wind blew across the water, two of them vanished. I assumed they were snuggling down in the burrow until I came home late from a party and found Blackberry sitting on the front doorstep waiting for me. He waited while I scrambled up a meal and then ate the whole panful.

Amber watched through the window, but I noticed she did not swell up like a balloon and hiss and make that strange noise cats produce by knocking their teeth together and blowing out air. If Amber and I were out walking (she goes on a leash), Blackberry might be in the yard too, and they simply inspected each other and Blackberry drank some more water. But once or twice Blackberry suggested coming in the house, and Amber would hiss and growl and blow, for she wants exclusive ownership of the house.

And once Blackberry drove off a big stray tiger cat. He made no effort to lift his elegant plume and spray her. He thumped the ground with his forepaws in a steady rhythm, backed up three steps, thumped again, and uttered a warning cry like a squeaky wheel. He also hissed. After a few moments, the cat walked away with great dignity. Blackberry gave one final thump and waded right into the middle of his pan, firmly establishing his territorial rights.

Much later a strange skunk came by, and Blackberry used the same tactics. The interloper thumped back and they poked their noses fiercely at each other, backed up and thumped, and gave the same eerie cry. It was all face to face with no sign of either's using the spray weapon.

I learned that when Blackberry is afraid he runs away. Apparently the only time he would use his deadly weapon would be to protect his life if he were attacked. He is no aggressor.

Birds he ignores, even when they dip their beaks in his own dish. The birds also ignore him, from the shy cardinals to the quail and mourning doves and all the rest. The bird feeder is near Blackberry's dish, and I can look out of the kitchen window and see a yard jammed with birds, with one busy skunk in their midst.

In the beginning he ate at dusk or later but gradually began to come earlier and earlier, and when he was hungry, he moved in circles around and around the yard, closer and closer to the door and always looking in at me with his shiny black eyes wistful. Sometimes he got hungry again around nine at night and said so. Amber would announce his arrival by flitting from window to window and peering out.

So now I take out another meal if he wants it at night. One night he even turned up around midnight, simply starving.

Life with a skunk is not an idle one. Every morning the water bowl has to be scrubbed and filled. Yesterday's cake pan comes in for a soak and wash. By mid-afternoon I get his dinner ready. And, of course, I have to shop for him. He drinks a great deal of milk or cream, eats as much canned cat food as I give him, and cat kibbles. But unlike my fussy Amber, he will eat any brand of fish and any kind of cheese. He also loves cut up bacon (cooked), chicken, beef, veal, lamb, ham, crumbled stale bread. He will eat some of the asparagus tips Amber leaves but is not crazy about them.

For dessert he ambles around the lawn, opening up anthills and eating the ants. He will happily dig up any plant just put in the garden and takes care of the grubs as well as killing the plant. I had heard skunks ate mice, but one poor dead field mouse in the yard he paid no attention to. He left me to gather it up gently and dispose of it.

When he first adopted me, I wondered whether he was a male, but as time went on and he never appeared with a few small kits, I felt he was not destined to become a mother. They breed, I am told, in February, and I watched anxiously during the subsequent months but his shape never did change.

I call him Kitty when I greet him, and if I am putting out his food early, I stand by the rail fence and summon him and wait until the wedge-shaped muzzle pokes up through the high grass. In full sun he does not see very well, but his nose monitors everything, and he weaves his head back and forth and sniffs. When he knows I am there, he hops toward me.

The movement of a skunk is hard to describe. He seems to amble from side to side as if he were heavy, but he can run fairly fast if anything scares him, lifting his sharply pointed paws rapidly, almost like a gallop. He sometimes, when just sauntering around, gives a little skip. I do not offer to pick him up, because I know Amber would take a dim view of this, since she had hysterics the one time I picked up a very small visiting puppy. But I am sure I could pick him up as far as he is concerned.

Special guests who stand at the window, endlessly admiring him, have the privilege of taking him a snack, and this is interesting, for he knows it is safe enough but does not want a stranger too near and hides until the yard is empty. He goes just far enough down the bank to feel invisible, but you can see his elegant ermine hood and ebony nose tip plainly. When I go out, he just stands around sniffing hungrily.

The relationship of people and animals is interesting to observe. My yard boy, for instance, is over six feet tall and was paralyzed with fright when he first saw the small creature in the yard. At first he stayed in his car until Blackberry went away. One day, finally, he bravely ventured to walk across the yard, tiptoeing nervously and sweating a bit. Then one day he said, "You know, he's pretty, isn't he?" And one day he said, "Can't I take Blackberry's dinner out?" As he went through the door, he added, "I could eat that myself— it sure looks good." Now he comes to the kitchen to see if dinner is in the pan so he can be the one who takes it out and calls, "Kitty, Kitty!"

It was deep winter when I had to go inland and Blackberry was supposed to be hibernating—although skunks only semihibernate, as I know because their tracks may be seen sometimes on a new fall of snow. The tracks are rather like those of a cat, but there is a blob behind them where the plume drags. A skunk evidently does not run with its tail erect but finds it more comfortable to let the tail sag.

I came back on a cold day toward the end of March, and the first thing I saw, before the car was even unloaded, was a familiar chunky ball of ermine and ebony, and a person who greeted me with the news that he was hungry. The unloading had to wait until I opened three cans of kitty tuna and found some evaporated milk to add.

In most animal relationships, one receives more than one gives. With wild animals, the sense of friendliness is heart warming. Learning so much about skunks has been a joy. And just the feeling that Blackberry trusts one of a deadly-enemy race makes me walk with pride.

From the experts I find out a good many facts but not enough. The burrow I see has a wide opening and goes in about four feet before turning. There is a separate part farther in, which is reserved for a bathroom. When it fills up, the skunk walls it off and digs a new one so the main burrow is clean. I learn that skunks may roam but keep the home place. Blackberry scoops out a fresh fall of dirt at the entrance occasionally.

Skunks come out now and then to forage. They breed early—around February. I imagine this is so that the kits may find insects and grubs abounding when they are old enough to be on their own. When they first emerge from the burrow, they follow their mother in a line, and she keeps track of them. They weigh, I believe, only a few ounces in the beginning, and I am sure Blackberry does not weigh much even now, although his thick lustrous coat makes him seem quite large.

Basically the skunk is nocturnal, but Blackberry does not pay any attention to that fact. Blackberry blinks his small shining eyes when he is out in the sun and sniffs constantly. He has a keen sense of smell and hearing. He can hear me open the front door, even if he is far down the bank, and begins to scrabble up. I also think he has a sixth sense, for he knows when an enemy is coming even when there is no sound at all. And I may be imagining it, but I am sure he knows the distinctive note my car motor makes, for when any other car drives in the driveway, he vanishes. When I drive in, he stands and waits and pays no attention when I bang the door.

I do not believe in trying to make any wild animal adopt mankind's pattern. I would never wish to restrain Blackberry or limit him to being a house pet. He should have his freedom to be what he is and follow his own dream. But it is possible to have a relationship with almost any wild creature without imposing on it, with much benefit to both. Descented skunks may be house trained and led out on a leash, but I would never subject Blackberry to this kind of life. I am satisfied to feed him, visit with him, chase stray dog packs away from his bank, and let him be himself.

As he lopes around the yard at sunset, we both feel this is the best of all worlds.

I had rolled the previous page from the typewriter around nine o'clock at night. I went into the front part of the house just to see if the pears in the kitchen were really ripe enough to try. Suddenly Amber began leaping from window to window and swelling up as only she can do. The old phrase "her hair stood on end" describes her at such moments, and nobody would guess she weighs only five pounds.

So I turned the yard light on and opened the inner front door. About six feet away stood a magnificent raccoon. Paralyzed with fright, he stared at me and then thumped the ground and swelled up about like my kitten. But what interested me most was that Blackberry had come back for a late snack and was nose down in the pie pan. The two of them were perhaps three feet apart, and obviously the visitor had been eating all the leftovers around the pan. And while I stood quietly, Blackberry obviously communicated somehow.

"Don't mind her; she's with it," is what he said, and went on eating.

Now I learned that a skunk and a coon can get along very well and that Blackberry was willing to share food with the coon as long as his own dish was not invaded. He fixed that problem by standing in the middle of his pan, paws firm.

I turned out the light and closed the door so the raccoon could calm down. I explained the situation to Amber and advised her not to climb the new, hideously expensive, drapes at the picture window.

Then I sat down and thought it over and decided I would double the food put out daily but would not make a personal friend of the coon, since I remembered the one time Amber snipped out of the door and attacked two coons who were on the lawn. She does not mind Blackberry sitting by the front door if I am late with dinner, but obviously a coon is a different matter.

After the ripeness of summer and the busyness of fall chores, there comes a special enchantment to New England as our valleys and hills blaze with scarlet and gold. Every season has her own beauty, from the delicate snowdrops blossoming at winter's end, with snow about their pale green stems, to the etched beauty of dark branches against a sky like blue ice in January, but October sings with color. And the air smells of windfall apples and the musty sweet of pumpkins and squash. The first leaves that turn have a lovely faint scent, and I always pick a few and hold them to my nose and just *sniff!*

Nights are crisp, and we keep the fire burning in the ancient fireplace, but days are warm gold, so picnics are still possible. There is a dark stillness about the pond which rests the spirit as we sit with our mugs of hot coffee and decide washing the storm windows can be put off awhile. My experience, after long country living, is that schedules can be flexible, and tomorrow is soon enough to start replenishing the woodpile and cleaning up the garden. Meanwhile, why not take a ride over some of the yet-quiet country roads and say hello to the old houses tucked in folds of the hills? There are still free-running brooks and ponds and meadows and woods, although the great highways are slicing our rural countryside into black ribbons.

Also, we still have our beloved wildlife. Curt went up past the old apple orchard this weekend and met a young buck deer, and I saw a bobcat running along the edge of the swamp. Bobcats were almost exterminated at one period, but here was this beautiful cat, moving with elegant grace. A bobcat does not run like a dog with fore feet and back feet two by two, as it were, but sets the back paws in the print of the front ones so there is a single track. The head is a blocky wedge, the rump slightly high, and my bobcat was what I call a chocolate gray with dark spots.

Bobcats eat rodents, moles, and some rabbits, but except when they are starving, they do not kill chickens unless the chickens are running loose far from a house, for bobcats are shy and simply want to live quietly, preferably in caves in rocky ledges, and raise their kittens far from mankind. They are important in the balance of nature and should not be killed off. They do not attack men or dogs except in self-defense. I would have liked to go out and speak to the one in our back yard but could not get out fast enough.

I am sad to think man is the real predator and destroyer of all living creatures. When we came to Stillmeadow, the mourning doves, mink, otter, most of the deer, all the ruffed grouse had been virtually wiped out. Finally the state enacted some protective laws, and now I can look out any morning and see the iridescent mourning doves popping the cracked corn in their mouths and occasionally watch a bevy of ruffed grouse moving with their stately gait toward the swamp. A few otter live in the stream, and sometimes my farmer neighbor sees a mink, but I have never been so fortunate.

Amber enjoys the skunks and coons that come for snacks at the well house, although a big stray dog will send her fur in all directions. On Cape Cod, she and I watched while the three skunks ate dinner, and chickadees and mockingbirds sit on the fence talking things over. Sometimes a couple of rabbits join us and in late afternoon some quail. The pheasants are more shy, but there is one who insists on running ahead of the car when I drive out, so the speed limit on Blue Rock Road has been lowered to three miles per hour.

The high point of autumn for all of us is when the geese fly over, their beautiful flight a dark V against the sapphire early-morning sky or in the white light of the moon. We country folk have a passionate love of the wild geese, perhaps because they are special evidence of the mystery of nature herself. They always have a leader who pilots the flock, and there are always one or two who trail behind trying to keep up. They mate for life, a fact I wish hunters would remember as they go gunning, for when the mate is killed a lonely goose is left behind.

Meals are simple now, because the out-of-doors is so enticing. One of our favorites is a dish I have shared with many friends, and I receive letters asking for it frequently all year long. (It is a good idea to keep a file in a box.) It is Connie's Kidney Bean Casserole, and we often have it for a buffet supper when neighbors come.

Here is the recipe for four. Mix 2 No. 2 cans kidney beans, drained; 3 small onions, cut fine; ½ green pepper, chopped; ¼ cup chopped ham (or more); and 1 small can tomato paste. Pour 1 cup red wine (Burgundy) over. Place in a greased casserole and lay bacon strips on top. Bake about 30 minutes in a moderate oven (350 degrees) or until it is bubbly. Serve with a mixed green salad and crusty garlic bread. Save the bean juice from the can to add to soups or stews.

If you keep ham on hand in the refrigerator as we always do, you can make this one-dish meal any time, using ingredients from the emergency shelf. Also, it does not require a long stay in the oven.

Incidentally, I am always sad when I see some of my friends drain the juice from cans and pour it down the sink. I save all vegetable juices for soups and fruit juices for desserts or compotes.

My mother brought me up to believe waste was practically sinful. Also, in much of her cooking she used chicken broth or beef instead of water or part stock with the water, which is one reason guests cleaned up the vegetable dishes. She was way ahead of her time, too, for she never drowned the asparagus in water but steamed it briefly so it kept its crisp green color and texture. Father used to bring in a basketful of wild asparagus, which loved the Wisconsin soil, and nothing could be more delicious.

Standard time begins the end of October, but nature herself sets her own time. When the summer birds begin to fly practice flights in skimming circles, it is not my clock that matters. The squirrels rush madly around gathering nuts. The chipmunks are ready to hibernate, and the skunks are getting as fat as possible. The first leaves drift down, and at night the Hunter's Moon sets her golden sail toward the horizon. I wear a warm jacket when I go out to say good night to the world and feel the air tastes of the long cold to come.

When company comes for a weekend, I am usually asked for Stillmeadow Onion Pie, which calls for 2 cups of flour, 2 teaspoons baking powder, ½ teaspoon salt, ⅓ cup shortening, ⅓ cup milk, 8 thinly sliced Bermuda onions, 3 tablespoons butter, salt and pepper to taste, 1 egg, ½ cup light cream, and broiled bacon strips.

Sift the dry ingredients together and cut in the shortening with a knife. Moisten with the milk. Mix the dough well and knead thoroughly. Cook the onions in a heavy skillet with the butter until golden but not brown. Press the dough into a 9-inch pie pan. When the onions are slightly cool, spread them thickly over the dough and sprinkle with salt and pepper. Beat the egg with the cream and pour the egg mixture over the onions. Bake about 20 minutes at 450 degrees or until the biscuit shell is crisp and brown at the edges and the filling slightly brown. Cover the top with broiled bacon slices and serve hot. Serves four to six.

This is our favorite supper dish on a crisp autumn night. We serve it with a tossed salad and fresh fruit for dessert.

On a dark windy day when we sit around the fire, we like Spanish Chocolate. For this you need 2 cups milk, 2 cups strong coffee, 2 squares bitter chocolate, grated (or ½ cup cocoa), 3 tablespoons sugar, and ½ teaspoon vanilla.

Bring the milk and coffee to a boil together, then stir in the grated chocolate or cocoa, add the sugar and vanilla, and whip until frothy. Serve in chocolate cups if you have them, or in mugs. We have some brown pottery mugs which are perfect for this.

Autumn rains are often as fierce as the assault of a legendary dragon. The colored leaves fall like jewels from a broken necklace. The swamp, which has seemed almost dry enough to walk on in August, now begins to stand knee-deep in water. A few weakened branches fall from the maples, and if the wind becomes a gale, one pine in the back yard always lets a few lower branches fall.

One of our personal mysteries is why this pine loses branches in wind or sleet or heavy snow while the others, planted at the same time and right near it, seldom give in. No tree man has ever been able to explain it.

Most of us, I believe, have inner barometers; certainly I do. During an autumn storm mine is very low. My movements slow, and I have a tendency to sit by the fire and just wait for the rain to stop even if what I had planned to do does not involve going outdoors. I listen to the wind, and I think melancholy thoughts. A three-day nor'easter induces me to disbelieve in the blue of the sky above the black clouds.

My father never cured me of this. He was one of those who loved great storms, wind, rain, sleet. He felt, for one thing, that they were a challenge, and for another, he was a geologist and loved to study any occurrence in nature. He would fly out, coat unbuttoned, in the worst storm and come in exploding with excitement, his red hair dripping or frosted with snow.

I now do appreciate the blessings of rain and snow and ice. I have lived through some disastrous droughts when prayers for rain went up like mist to the heavens. The earth could not long survive or give life to us without rain. Everything in nature depends on enough precipitation, as the weathermen call it. Without rainfall or snow melt, the water table is lowered, and even the steel and stone urban centers begin to ration water.

But in New England we may have days of rain, especially in late fall.

And one day when I finally got to the market, I said I was thankful we were having such good rain, thankful it would brim the ponds, restore the brooks, nourish the earth, sink down to the deepest roots of the tallest trees.

But I added, as I picked up my groceries, "Well, sometimes I get tired of being thankful!"

My idea would be for it to rain at night and then clear with the sun, making diamonds of every drop on every leaf. Or one day now and then, rain with a steady silvery-gray rain, which would stop at sunset or at least when the transparent young moon might come out.

I admire my dear friends Helen, Vicky, and Olive, who may be sitting by the fire with me on a dark day while the rain lashes the windows. They will simultaneously get a gleam in their eyes, and Helen will say, "It would be nice to *take one more walk today*."

They not only fly out like a flock of birds but come in ecstatic. And as if that were not bad enough, they will also plunge out in a heavy snow, and when I peer through the window, I see their diminished figures vanishing toward Jeremy Swamp.

I put another log on the fire and make a hot toddy and get my exercise for the day brushing Amber. For Amber, at least, agrees with me about everything and feels nobody should so much as put one paw outside unless the sun is shining.

I have difficulty in autumn as the days grow shorter even if there is no storm. When it is dark by four in the afternoon, I feel it must be time to start dinner. And I expect this shows I do not really live by the clock but by light and dark. When it is time to turn on all the lights, I am usually puttering around in the kitchen, with the result that supper is ready an hour before anyone else in the family is willing to eat. Then it follows that once it is authentically night, I am in fine shape because it *should* be night. By the time everyone in the house is ready for bed, I am sparkling. But little pieces of night tossed into what should be day just upset me.

It proves that I cannot really live by clocks, although we have them in every room of the house. Often when time drops an hour or gains one, I forget to set the clocks back or forward and may go a week a full hour off the schedule of the more compliant folk. I do wish the government would have one time all year and keep it.

I measure time by nature, and when the dark-red oak leaves finally fall, defeated by wind and rain, I know another season is over. The chickadees and juncos will be residents from now on, and a few nuthatches who run head-down on the maple tree trunks. The wild geese have gone over, sounding their mysterious cry, which has never been accurately described, for it is mournful and yet oddly triumphant and exciting.

In New England, people are planning to go to Florida—or to some island or to visit relatives in California. But a good many of us simply batten down, as we say, and spend time at the market explaining *why* we are not going away. This compulsion to go may be peculiar to Americans, but I am always amazed when some of my friends feel they must apologize if they stay in the valley the year round. One of my dearest friends felt she was important only when she finally made the grand tour of Europe, although I gathered afterward she was uncomfortable most of the time.

As for me, I agree with William Hazlitt, who wrote in 1824, "I should like to spend the whole of my life in traveling abroad, if I could anywhere borrow another life to spend afterwards at home."

I did once go to Europe, but it was before my roots had gone down. And Jill spent a year or more studying in Vienna, but once she got back, she never once said casually, "Well, when I was in Vienna—"

Travel is broadening, I know. And I certainly learned a lot, including how seasick one can get on an ocean linner. I cherish many memories, such as visiting Keats's house in Hampstead and standing right in the room where he wrote poetry I have lived by since I was fifteen.

But I never understand people who write me how dull their lives are because they never get anywhere. Every day is an experience in living wherever you are, and those of us who survive the New England winters have a special pride in managing when "the electric" goes off, the pipes freeze, the roads are unplowed, and the thermometer skates down to thirty below. In a period when people are so often just numbers, we feel the security of being persons, and we walk proudly.

And then who can appreciate the arrival of the redwings as we do, with the "Okalee, Okalee" sounding in the maples, and that day in March when the yard has little mounds of cold black earth where the earthworms are announcing winter has not killed them. And there are the first purple crocus opening when winter is still reluctant to go.

As long as you have a window, life is exciting.

My travel is limited to going to Cape Cod part of the year, and this can hardly be compared to going to Greece or a South Sea Island, for the house on Mill Pond is merely an extension of Stillmeadow, and getting there just involves packing Amber's litter tray and carrying case and vitamins and a couple of cartons of my manuscripts. And about the only major change is getting used to the fact that Channel 13 on the TV is now Channel 2.

And, of course, the skunks I feed on the Cape have different names from those I feed at the farm. But they all eat as much—and they get fed no matter which place I am in.

The summer birds are gone, and this mean it is time to stock the big can of birdseed by the back door and be ready to wait on the winter boarders who do not migrate. After a snowfall, the air is full of wings, from the tiny chickadee friends to the flaming bright cardinals, the delicate juncos, the sea-blue jays. The Canadian geese go over, uttering their lost, lonely cry. Squirrels seem to fly, too, as they leap from tree to tree. The raccoons and skunks come for their handouts.

The first gold and garnet leaves drift down and paint the pond with color. When the lawn mower is put away, the yard will be deep with more and more leaves. I like to walk in them, smelling the dark, spicy scent. They will nourish the earth as they disintegrate, for nothing is lost in nature as the seasons turn.

The exuberance of spring is over, and the rich ripeness of summer is gone. The extravagant beauty of October fades into the sober hue of November, and once more the trees will lift intricate patterns of dark branches against a soft pale sky.

The early morning is crisp and still smells of windfall apples. At dusk we smell the mist silvering the swamp. And if we go out when the moon rises, we breathe air like wine.

It is not an ending as a season draws to a close but only a beginning of a new time. Erwin brings in a fresh load of seasoned logs for the fire, which now burns from breakfast to bedtime.

And I turn a fresh page in my journal because every day brings a new experience.

THE END